Anniecat Chro

Anniecat Chronicles

Joan Rust

Copyright © 2014 by Joan Rust.

ISBN: Softcover   978-1-4931-8686-0

                  eBook   978-1-4931-8687-7

This book was printed in the United States of America.

Rev. date: 03/27/2014

To order additional copies of this book, contact:
Xlibris LLC
1-888-795-4274
www.Xlibris.com
Orders@Xlibris.com
611978

For my children:

        Tom Beggs

        Jeffrey Beggs

        Kimberly Beggs

        Scott Beggs

                with enormous love and admiration

Dear Barbara,

Remember before Dave Barry and Ann Landers when "Comings, Goings and Events" was the column we turned to first in the *Sault Evening News*? We could learn who had visitors from faraway places such as Newberry or Trout Lake. Bridal and baby showers, vacation trips and hospital bulletins were reported in a column of small paragraphs running the length of an inside page. You told me your Aunt Minetta was one of the correspondents from outlying areas who would submit news in exchange for free newspaper delivery. And we always read "50 Years Ago Today." Didn't it seem as if we were reading about another era . . . not really unimaginable, but certainly pre-us? We were astonished when we recognized a name under those old photographs, their torn corners and creases more clearly reproduced than the images gazing at us from the past. Our curiosity would then move us to count the rows in a group, moving l. to r., and we would focus on a face as if establishing some hazy link with another time.

Fifty years ago is now a comfortable and frequent topic for our conversation. The children and grandchildren look to us for the details of their beginnings. Genealogy searches cannot call forth the events and faces of our ancestry like a good story. As well, there is no better way to recall our own ancient history or to enhance today than by sharing memories, secrets, random thoughts and Coming, Goings and Events with a friend of more than 50 Years Ago Today. I will hope to assemble our letters into some form of chronicle of the fun we had growing up and beyond the Soo to Stonington and Beaufort.

A final thought . . . In the event a newspaper should want one for an historical photo, keep a good group shot including us in a place where the children will find it. We must DESTROY NOW the 1950 snapshot of us posing on the beach at Birch Point with our white cotton underpants rolled down to look like a bikini and our training bras stuffed with Kleenex. If you look closely, you'll see we are standing on tiptoe, as if ready to launch ourselves at a most daring and positive moment . . . into the Great Adventures we knew were out there. Happy 80th year dear friend and fellow great adventurer. love, jo

Hah Jo, you cannot rewrite history! I am hanging on to the picture of previous questionable behavior! Do you know how they always have pics of the deceased by the casket? Well, I am sending all your children a framed copy of that infamous photo so that it can be sitting right up there by the daisies from your quilting circle. Little Henrik will say: "Wow, Grandma was a swinger." No matter how you cut it, Jesus knows we did it. The devil made us. Love from

Barbara of Beautiful Beaufort

Anniecat Chronicles

1999.10.1   Meet anniecat

Let me introduce anniecat who first came to my door during a serious blizzard three years ago in January. My friend Ace was here for our annual Chinese takeout and Scrabble tournament; and, in addition to having uncanny luck with board games, she also has asthma. When annie's frosty face appeared at the window, I knew, therefore, that inviting a cat to share the evening with us was a bad idea. I put a dish of warm milk and leftover Chinese out the door that night. Thus, the ground rules were laid for what became a very satisfying arrangement for the stray kitten and me. I would feed her, and she would remain outdoors. The plucky little creature ate this first offering and retreated into the storm, returning each evening at what she deemed her dinner hour. The bargain struck, annie happily lives her wild life in the woods, and I continue mine, semi-petless. She is a convenient cat, and never makes any demands on me except for the small dish of bottom shelf WalMart cat food which supplements her mysterious diet. She is also a beautiful animal, perhaps large part Himalayan, with incredible blue eyes, and a demeanor which discourages familiarity. Friends who come to visit hope for just a sighting, and perhaps she will come as far as the deck if they are reasonably sober and patient. But with me, she is a loving, purring, rubbing, warm and snuggling friend. She brought me her two firstborn babies to care for, and was rewarded with a trip in a cage to the vet for surgery; and so, she is also forgiving, especially because the little ones were immediately whisked off for adoption. This event led to her name because I took her to a bureaucratic vet who needed a Name for the Animal. The granddaughters said she should be Orphan Annie. The cat said she preferred "anniecat" . . . dropping the Orphan, which she wasn't and adding the cat, which she was.

The foliage is dropping from the trees, leaving our little world in the Stonington hardwoods more open and exposed daily, and anniecat Who Prefers to Live In The Woods is adjusting to this lack of cover by appearing at the door only after sunset until she takes up winter residence in the ceiling insulation of the garage, an amendment to our original agreement. She hasn't heard of Scottsdale or Boca, so probably considers herself lucky indeed to be able to "get away for the winter." A kitty portal was installed for her convenience and safety, and Auntie Carol and Uncle Ken were recruited to fill her dish in my absence, a thankless job. I was gone two months last winter, and she did not show herself to them once. However, during this past year she has ventured into the house to sit with me in the evenings, two middle-aged ladies now, enjoying comfort, warmth and company. Perhaps it is time for both of us to give up our wild ways. I tell everyone anniecat handles the email because she is "litter-ate" and thus our address. She thanks you for asking about her, but reminds you she does not accept invitations or requests. Nevertheless, regards from jojo and anniecat

2000.5.18   Logging On

Dear mothagoose@ . . . .

The weather is finally stable enough to drag my favorite old "deck" chair from winter storage in the garden shed. I can spend time now sitting outdoors with books and my thoughts while enjoying the new activity along the shore of Little Bay de Noc. My two sandhill cranes are back, this year accompanied by a third party whose relationship to the pair is worthy of speculation. I think about this, but find three cranes and most other concerns vanish with a nice nap. Has anyone else considered how the first touch of unobstructed sunshine on our winter-chilled bodies can revive us . . . and then lull us into a sighing, restful doze? My children would say the fumes from the ancient chair have overcome me . . . the familiar scent of old sun oil, winter damp and a whisper of mice. Isn't it the ordinary, as well as new mysteries, combined with our awareness of the moment which inspire you and me and our like to journal these little events from our lives?

I look forward to your letters from South Carolina. Do you tell anyone you are from **northern** Michigan? Perhaps you should just gradually infiltrate the congregation at the Baptist Church of Beaufort. All those historical novels we have read may ease you into the conversation at neighborhood oyster roasts. I do understand, Burba, that the reverence for history in your new surroundings is hard-earned, however. You and Earl are probably already touring, reading and taking root in southern soil. What was it you quoted: "We weren't born in the South, but we got here as soon as we could." I promise to keep you in touch with Yooper life. I am anniecat@ . . . . love from jojo

2000.7.10   At Home in Beaufort

It is hot here, but we have no problems enjoying it. The house stays at one AC temperature all the time. The bedroom is opened to the porches at night. We use one of the porches for coffee in the morning and drinks or dinner or both in the evening. A breeze comes up about 5 p.m. and, through a lucky chance, our house faces the prevailing winds . . . which are south in Beaufort. The porch facing north will be a winter retreat, and has a swing. I am learning to deal with the flora and fauna and other things. The beach and ocean are wonderful. Earl is pulling in blue crabs from in front of the house and is learning to throw a shrimp net. Right now the ocean is warm as toast, meaning the first hurricane should be getting organized and so are we with lists of what to do. Mainly, we are lucky we have our RV nearby. We are really enjoying new people, learning new things, new joys (hymns at the Baptist church)and a comfortable place to rest each night and recover from all of the above. Love, Barbara

2000.8.13

All I have on my list this week is trim the oleanders and get iron for the gardenia bushes. Must I dig up a railroad track and bring it home to bury? I am seriously too old to take up southern gardening. I am probably putting an able-bodied illegal person out of work. Do we have plumbago in the north? Do you know I have to plant pansies when it gets cold and they last all winter? There is no rest here while snow birds fly away. Gardening goes on month in and month out. I never thought about such an unexpectedly laborious situation. We are flying the Packer flag today and awaiting the game at 4 p.m. We should really be at the beach doing push-ups in the sand. I will look for pictures of the house to send you. Love, mothagoose and the Earl

2000.8.15   Thumbing Through "Southern Living"

Jo: For years now, I have only been thumbing my
way through "Southern Living" in the checkout
line at Piggly Wiggly. For example, I totally
missed the article on how to trim your great
grandmother's Christmas cactus into a life size
statue of Robert E. Lee. (Don't get confused.
I know this same item also ran in the July
issue of "Martha Stewart Living." What I have
been doing is grooving on the more photographic
issues of "Coastal Living." Recently I spent a
lot of time viewing the Cabot-Stimpson-Reynolds
family having a 16 course oyster roast in the
sand at Nags Head wearing nothing but thin
white dresses. Accordingly, spider mites ate my
oleanders.

Love, Beaufort Barb

2000.9.12

Burba, Okay, now send me pictures of your real house! The scenes I
received look like a photo shoot for your aforementioned "Southern
Living" research. What a beautiful, beautiful home. And with
blooming flora and a big ol' porch swing. Am so happy for you and
Earl. Can just see you on the porch sipping something refreshing. Oh,
wait . . . is that an entire pitcher of cool beverage I see in one view?
Thank you for brightening my day. Looking forward to the Knowles
Island "camp" which promises an immersion in the history of your
area in SC while offering naturalist experience. I will be down the
road from you in February after visiting with Scott in Lauderdale.
As I recall my camping in Alaska with a similar group, I see myself
arriving at your door thin, sleep deprived and snake bit. Make that a
large pitcher of refreshments! jojo

2000.8.27   Knowles Island

Oh Jo: What a deal! I am waiting for my neighbor
to get home to give me a fix on Knowles Island.
There are about a million islands here, however.
I think that maybe a friend's daughter who is
married to a man who is assistant to a famous
movie star everyone knows but me has a brother
that lives near or on that island. It is a
lovely area. You will fall in love. I think you
should come here first because it is cold that
time of year and you can make the adjustment
from Florida and sit by our fire and watch the
tides, the birds, the cotton rats. It will give
you some background for your classes. What do
you think?? We will feed you low country food
so that you can be the star in the cuisine
class. We will also give you a blanket for your
bed. Please come for lots of days before your
conference starts and enjoy exploring our marsh.
Some nights, tucked under your blanket, you
will hear gulub gulub which will be the high
winter tides coming to tell you how foolish your
friends were to build at sea level three.

I am really excited about your visit. Is it
February yet? Will you be here soon? Love,
Barbara

2000.11.30   Election Results

Burba, I love all these foreign governments who have jumped in
during the wee hours to be the first to cozy up to the new Pres. with
congratulations (and requests for new trade agreements, out and out
aid, arms exchanges, etc.) only to find that perhaps the other guy may
win. Well, anyway, I'm still planning my trip to Florida in January,

even though the State Election Commission may run the state by then. Since we have memorized all the Frank Yerby novels, we can now satisfy our appetites for new heroes and heroines in Love and Danger by emptying the shelves of Wilbur Smith's books. Is there anything that proves a friendship like the way we interpret a story?? jojo

01.2.10   Reviewing Wilbur Smith

Oh, Jo: No sooner had Miss Sunshine jumped from the sinking Red Cross ship than she fed a poor old sailor to the sharks. I did not forget that the submarine captain has an unmentionable son. And who will that be? Surely no relative of this little old man and the women that Centaine is running across Africa with! I have to keep in mind that if Centaine ever meets up with Lothar and marries him, she will be Centaine de Thiry de la Rey. I refuse to pay for monogramming her sheets. We are heading for the beach for a week. Earl is off to the library to get a Wilbur Smith book for himself. It will be fun to trade off with him. BofBB

P.S. Centaine de Thiry has just gotten herself pg out of wedlock, watched her boyfriend fry, watched Daddy repeat the act, lost her horse in a bloody bomb attack, lost her childhood home to fire and, in what seems to be a few days, has recovered enough to be known as Miss Sunshine, the Red Cross Nurse. Are you trying to give me the message that I should laugh in the face of adversity along with Centaine? Or do you want me to try for Lothar De La Rey, the bold and cruel gunrunner? Can Centaine get pregnant twice in one day? Can the one-legged twin love her as much as the two-legged-but-limps twin? Gotta go. Gotta read.

01.3.10   Yooper Guilt

One week before St. Patrick's Day, and the weather is disturbingly warm and sunny. The temperatures have soared into the 50's. Rust begins to creep across the idle shovels as robin sightings multiply. Fear is building. The storm is coming.

Yooper guilt is Biblical on sunny days. This fact is not entirely attributable to the Lutherans, although they have tried their best to stir up a little fear at coffee hour when things are going too well. Simply, we believe we do not deserve good weather; and as balmy breezes blow across Stonington, we keep expecting another one or two blizzards . . . . or at least a good tornado. Yoopers have their winter jackets hanging in the front closet all summer.

In the Upper Peninsula of Michigan, where temperatures can range from 20 degrees below zero to the nineties above, talking about the weather is not just idle conversation. Who doesn't know that if the January temperature stays above zero, we could have a bad flu season; thus, a good "cold snap" kills off serious virus. Too much rain will rot the hayfields, too little will ruin the blueberries. We all have our favorite meteorologist, each elevated to rock star status.

However, fearful as we can be on good days, we are philosophical on bad ones. We tell each other how lucky we are there are no earthquakes north of the Mackinac Bridge, as we tunnel through snowdrifts on the sixth consecutive day. We extol our good fortune in escaping hurricanes while trees crash around us in gales off Lake Superior. We are grateful that we don't have to battle city traffic even as we slide off the icy road into the woods. Toasting marshmallows on a summer campfire, children hear stories of historic hard winters.

Some claim global warming is affecting Yooper weather guilt. The old-timers say we don't have bad winters anymore; and zone heating, snowblowers or months in Florida have taken the edge off our fear of what is imminent. A new generation just doesn't seem to worry ahead like we used to. But the week of St. Patrick's Day remains legend. Winter saves its worst for last in the Upper Peninsula. Days of bright sunshine, melting snow, open water in the bay could lull the innocents into spring fever. However, the truly guilty Yoopers know what could be the weather of the century is due. We buy our corned beef a week early; and fortifying ourselves with green Bud Lite, await the storm.

01.4.9   The Suitcase

Barb! What upsetting news! I just learned of Earl's surgery. This was a bit of a shock, but am so grateful that the doctors were "take action kind of guys." I have these terrible nightmares of him struggling up and down stairs with my SUITCASE, pursued by swat teams of surgeons!! Please assure him that I have purchased a very lightweight bag made of something manufactured on surplus carnival candy machines, and sold only to people who wear size 4 clothes. I will lose weight later, but I have to keep my suitcase somewhere cool. Love and restored health to him!

And it will be a relief to you to be able to be his friend again instead of his nurse. I was just about to express mail you cheerful pink scrubs and a pair of squeaky rubber-soled shoes. He is lucky to have you, and remember you are supposed to remind him of this all the time while he is in a weakened state. Enjoy the workouts and you will dazzle the old classmates with your bod, greatly softening the horror when I come lumbering in. jojo

My Dear Burba,

You have missed your calling. You must talk Earl into moving to New York with you where he will become The Donald's confidant on real estate and loaner cars and you can write. You and Earl will hang out in bistros, drink martinis, meet Regis, appear at the Tony awards in transparent shirts. You could talk Earl into moving to Hollywood where he will buy and sell spa resorts and you can do screenplays of all Frank Yerby's works or write short acceptance speeches for Julia Roberts. You two will eat at vegetarian bistros, drink wine straight and wear transparent shirts and pants to the Oscar awards. Your Dexter Dog and I will be so proud. Seriously, you both are such clever writers . . . and I want you to know that I laughed so hard at the one act play I about scared poor anniecat out of the rafters. On second thought . . . just write for your friends. Each letter is a present. your jojo and anniescardeycat

01.4.20   New Hip

Burba, Just to let you know . . . My nurses, Ken and Carol, have removed my bib and I am home to my own house with the new hip. I went in to have my staples removed and nothing fell off. I think the surgeon scribbled "salvaged" or "recycled" on my chart, and said I was doing well. He looked as if he wanted to modify this last statement as he watched me crashing away down the hall on the new crutches. In our initial consultation, he told me I could expect a good result. I took this to mean I will eventually be able to climb out of a kayak instead of rolling out into the shallows like an old walrus, thus lending my own interpretation to the kayaking term "Eskimo Roll." jojo

01.5.21   Hopalong Housebound

Burba: Hope all is going well with Earl's cardio recovery. Earl riding in the back seat must have been a difficult stage for both of you. I know I am looking forward to just getting in the car and driving off to pick up a gallon of milk, returning my books to the library or merely enjoying the scenery beyond my driveway. I have had to put such things off as if they were trips to another planet. Am doing well, however, and nearly 4 weeks post op . . . last visit this week from the home health nurses and their sadistic little blood draws. My skin is still molting from the bad experience with Keflex, and I am limited to slippers on my swollen toes. If things don't improve a whole lot before the reunion, I may have to go barefoot, covered in a sari, claiming I was the Class of '51 exchange student. Meanwhile, I am cutting a path through my book list, keeping everything at waist level shipshape, and learning new uses for long Bar-B-Q tongs every day. I am sorta like Edward Scissorhands, but have to remember to rinse off the tongs before I use them for turning the bratwurst. Here I am back at the computer in the garage. I left the house at sunrise, and made it out here before noon. Now, to go back. I think I should have packed a lunch. Actually doing pretty well with the crutches. I have a whole new respect for Tiny Tim Cratchett whose family could only afford one crutch for him. Keep up the good work Earl and Nurse Barbara. Am starting back to the house now, hoping to get back in time for the Market Wrap this afternoon. jojo

01.6.10   Camping Near the Wyeths

Jo, Earl and I are very enthused about your idea of dressing as an exchange student. I think with a sari and bare feet the renowned barrette from your old boyfriend we both admire should go in your nose. This will halt the need for a '50's style hairdo. Just so you don't feel alone, I will wear long underwear below my dress and go as a secret Upper Peninsula Finn. I am writing this to you from our campsite in N. South Carolina. Took us about four and a half hrs. to bring the RV here and get it parked. First, we selected a "Club" campground, but that suited us for only one night and we quickly returned to our favorite, the Corp. Parks. Very, very cheap—your tax dollars at work. (you did remember to send money this year didn't you?) Anyway, we drove into nearby Greenville which is lovely. We actually wanted to go to their art museum and see the Wyeths (largest collection in USA). They were having a special exhibit where they had brought in even more paintings for the summer, so we really got to see Andrew. Earl said he felt very humble when we walked out the door. Then we spent lots of time investigating downtown which is being recreated after the Mall that ate Main Street. When you stop spending money on country singers

and buy yourself a travel rig, we will have all
these good places listed for you. The parks are
about 7 to 9 dollars a night for us oldsters.
You can't afford to stay home for that price.

We will return to Beaufort 6/27 and then I must
get busy for my trip to Escanaba. Since your
children have decided to use your suitcase as
a cottage this summer, Earl bought me a hanging
bag for some of my clothes. I'm a packing
Grinch when it comes to suitcases, so the next
week probably will not be pretty. Do you have
a Who Is and Who Isn't Coming To The Reunion
List?

I have to go stir up the campfire now and cook
while watching Kudzu grow. Love, Mothagoose

01.6.9   Well Drillers and Poison Ivy

Jo: Have poison ivy covering face, nose, ears,
shoulders. Decided to go to the reunion as the
Future Nurses Club project. Have great need
to borrow the rhinestone barrette from our
old boyfriend to keep long, greasy strands of
hair out of running sores. Do you want to sit
with me at dinner or should I ask the class
Lothario? B

Burba , , , Didn't your Mama ever tell you not to pick poison ivy and
your nose at the same time?? I would suggest: (1) don't expect the
FNA to sponsor you—touchy about their reputations; try the Munchin
Moochers; and (2) isn't there some sort of redundancy between being
blemished and sitting next to Lothario. Not to worry , , , am sure by
the time the reunion rolls around, you will be lovely as ever. I am
doing fine with the new hip hardware, and walking well . . . . sort of. I
still have a slight list which is not noticeable if I walk along slopes. If I

don't correct this, and your sores are still draining by July, perhaps you and I could find a very shady spot on an incline where we could hang around.

01.6.17

Burba, Just when I had thought my house and yard were a real disaster area (should I notify FEMA??) The Delta County Health Dept. and I find that the time has come to drill a well. The permits filed, and agreements on site and how close to bankruptcy I want to go have been decided. The drillers will be here next week. First the tree people had to come and take out a lovely huge oak to allow the drilling rig to get by my house, placing me closer to the aforementioned bankruptcy and costing me emotionally as well. I fed the tree men lunch and fresh rhubarb pie, and they left firewood which I briefly considered selling in those neat little bundles to campers at the neighborhood campground. However, I am still placing pickle jugs in the local bars to solicit contributions to my well fund ("Help Jo Find The Flow"). Spaghetti supper benefit at a later date. Just pray we find water somewhere above the Yangtze River, Love to you both . . . . jojo

01.6.17   Preparing for the 50th Class Reunion and Well Digging

Burba: The well drillers disappointed me by postponing the well project until next week, which means they probably will show up about the time you arrive. Perhaps we will be drinking bottled water and skinnydipping in the middle of the night. I will pick you up at Escanaba International. I scheduled an appointment for you with a manicurist where I have my hairdo mowed. She speaks Yooper, so hope you won't be disappointed. The dermatologist removed some "sun spots" last week, and am waiting for my face to improve. Having had this done many times, the idea of a face peel never seems attractive to me. That lovely little barrette is going to have to carry a lot of weight if my face is blotchy, my legs still peeling from the hives, and my body leaning (to the right, of course). Let's pray for miracles, and you and I will manage to be real smashes. Or be really smashed . . . . This brings love from jojo

01.7.1

Burba, Yes, the drillers have been here, and I have a very nice well, indeed. However, the entire half of my lakefront property looks as if they dropped a bomb to find water rather than try conventional methods. And after I cooked 2 meat pizzas and fresh oatmeal cookies for the crew and faithfully brought jugs of ice water to them. But that is the way it is done everyone tells me as we then launch into discussions of who was left with the largest "sludge" pile from the drilling. I have called a landscaper to come and help me with the ruts left by the rig tires after I saw anniecat scaling the sides of one furrow as if it were Mt. Everest. I'm thinking my friends who drink Manhattans and have trouble even on level ground could wander off the deck and sue me when they are found sober at the bottom of a trench. I will have a house full for next week, the 4th of July, with kids plus one ex-husband-fishing buddy. Then I can start worrying about the fact that I haven't thought about what to wear for the class reunion. Can't tell you how I am looking forward to your visit. Have to run now and check the excavations for survivors. Love from jojo and anniehillarycat

01.7.10   Not Quite

Skirting the blueberry plains of the east, long stretches of Upper Michigan highways walled by dense forest eventually channel the rock of the Copper Country in the west, always finding their way back to touch the shorelines of the Great Lakes. During four months of the year, the safest place on U.P. roads is behind a snowplow. Notwithstanding this seasonal limitation, a trip along our roadways can be breathtaking with scenery, reassuring in its purity and, as I found on one trip, thought-provoking.

From outwardly deserted miles of road, driveways disappear into the landscape, each marked by property owners in varying degrees of carpentry and eloquence. From the always acceptable **Private Drive** and **No Trespassing**, Upper Michigan property signs are testament to the Yoopers' appreciation of all things outdoors and a tribute to their sense of humor. One family combined both on a clearing where a small camper and garden shed comprised the estate of **Manor Vista**. Lodge is a popular but ambitious word used on U.P. signposts. Often paired with **wilderness, timber** or **north country**, some of these properties are proof that every man's home near trees is his castle. The abundant and varied trees, alone, have inspired poetic landowners. Look for **Shady Oaks, Tall Pines, Whispering Willows**. Along the lakefronts, shores are **sunny, rocky, sandy**. Spending your vacation at a cottage named **Lazy Daze** sounds like a good idea; but, too, cabins and corners are **cozy**. Countless Packer shrines are everywhere despite the fact that few games can be televised into the woods four hours from Lambeau Field. Camp signs make fun viewing in areas of good hunting, and most contain the word **beer**. I notice every year **Camp Six Pack** records the largest deer kill in the newspaper's *Hunters' Report* while also maintaining their record contributions to recycling. Until recently, my vote for best U.P. property sign . . . no small distinction . . . was the proclamation **This Is It**. But it wasn't.

Traveling alone from Stonington to Marquette allows the driver opportunities to plan a schedule for the day . . . mentally selecting an uncommon place for lunch and sorting a list of stops by business and unexpired coupons. Once past Rapid River and the heavier logging traffic, the cruise control goes on, and, allowing for the impromptu deer crossings, one can cautiously enjoy the scenery. On a recent drive north, the familiar landmarks told me I was on schedule as I passed Trenary and began the long wooded curves away from the Whitefish River. Perhaps in the past I had missed the small sign in bad weather or traffic. Lettered by hand on yellow enameled board, it read **Not Quite**. Hanging from a piece of rusted pipe, it slanted comfortably toward the woods. Not quite . . . what? Traveling on to Marquette, my thoughts stayed at the roadside all morning trying to appreciate its message. Not quite a cottage, camp, lodge , , , manor? Was the property not quite paid for? Was the site said to be not quite to Marquette? The rough painted board and hand lettering showed a little cheek by leaving us with just two words. But the impermanence of the sign suited the optimism of the message . . . . *Not Quite*.

On the return trip, I slowed near the area where I had seen the small marker, and dropped behind traffic to allow a look down the driveway beyond it. There were no indications of habitation or hopeful activity visible. In fact, the two tracks leading into the trees were only faint impressions on a growth of tall grass bright with Indian paintbrush and buttercup. Perhaps the sign should be enlarged to read *Not Quite Yet* . . . . But, on a sunny day, heading home through the fresh color of the summer hardwoods, my final thought about the tilted yellow board came from nowhere. Whatever was down that beautifully overgrown trail was supposed to be not quite what anyone expected.

01.8.1   Reunion Afterglow

Burba, Thank you for the birthday greetings. I don't mind birthdays now that I am counting backwards. Have reached 19 again . . . my favorite year. All is forgiven for making such a hit with everyone at the reunion, including my old boyfriend. Was fun to have you here at my little place for a change, and to travel on to the Soo together. I think anniecat misses you. I know she missed me . . . we didn't leave enough food for her. Did Earl miss you? Did you tell him and Dexter Dog how we stayed up late at night, ate unhealthy food and drank Canadian beer?? Did you tell them that jojo wanted to keep you here longer because you are the best kind of friend? Love jojo and anniemalnourishedcat

P.S. I have unsettled thoughts about our reunion. Do reunions at this stage in our lives become gatherings where we look around and wonder who will be missing next time? I would not want to be there thinking that. Would be like some sort of farewell party each time. Or do we make sure we enjoy all the time we can with people we grew up caring about . . . knowing that time for all of us is precious. Let's go for it!!!!! Hugs until I see you. your, jojo

01.8.3   Birthday Burt's Bees

Glad you received the package before hurricane season. Please note waterproof packet enclosing useful and tasty supplies. My dealer makes no claims regarding the nutritional value of the Burt's Bees products, but I am delighted with the results I've had when I squirt some of the coconut foot cream in my pina colada mix. I thought the kit was a good idea for your condo(s), and hope you are enjoying enriched hair . . . Happy Birthday. Actually, I had noted this on a suitably obscene card which was to accompany your mailing. I sent out the water sample for my new well at the same time, and, when I read your letter, was a bit worried about the lady in the Public Health Department opening up the mail and finding a picture of ancient women practicing toilet squats at a gym. However, I found your card in the well drilling forms folder. I must check with Burt's Bees to see if he has something which will nourish my brain, remove calluses and tastes like mango.

I accepted an invitation to a committee "post-reunion party" I thought was very generous of the committee since I had only attended one meeting. So I drove up to the Soo this past Tuesday and checked in at Motel Todd. Maggie Dog, by the way, sends her regards; and would like you to know that she has that little problem with incontinence under control, thanks to some medication. I cooked for the kids one night, and was able to hold Parker Thomas Rutledge while Madeleine Rose and I painted with water in one of those magical little books where the colors appear when you wet down the pages. I am working at School Bell Crafts this afternoon, and will be there when the mysterious woodworker comes to pick up his wares. Our friends are intrigued by his life in the Stonington woods without electricity or other amenities. He does his beautiful woodworking using power from an old tractor. I will write and describe . . . or maybe not. Perhaps he is in the witness protection program, and once I actually see him the FBI will arrive to make me take some sort of oath or ship me to Hamtramack. If you don't hear from me again, here is the Burt's dealer address for your granddaughter. jo

01.8.7   Fair Week

Next week is Fair Week. Now is the time for Yoopers to add the following statement to all conversations: "When the fair is over, it seems as if that is the end of summer." A good saying because sometimes summer doesn't even wait for the fair to end before it does. My thoughts are turning to making the house wintersafe again; and the fellow who said he would be here in the spring to replace my doors has yet to appear. Perhaps I was mistaken about which spring he planned to do the work. You two have replaced major portions of your house, and I am still looking down the road for the carpenter's truck. Stay well and give my love to Beautiful Beaufort By The Sea. your jojo and anniecat

01.8.12   At Alan Jackson's Feet

Burba, This coming weekend I put on the lip gloss, best-loved boots and shirt with roses on it to join the crowd at Alan Jackson's feet. I have VIP tickets which will probably put me at eye level with one of the torn areas in his jeans. Dave is going with me to keep me out of jail.

Scotty comes in next week from Florida, and I am looking forward to having him around. The cousins will also be here; and so there will be potluck dinners and bonfires with marshmallows and Hershey bars. August is the time of star showers, and the grandchildren and I will plan a gathering on the beach to spread out on the blankets and look upward together, feeling for a short time that we are all the same size . . . . infinitesimal. Molly is home from music camp, and in her first phone call to me declared herself "dedicated to music," speaking as if she had taken a sacred vow and would now don some sort of habit/band uniform with gold braid. This is good. We were beginning to fear she was dedicated to boys or Abercrombie and Fitch or both. Hope all is well in Beautiful Beaufort by the Sea. If you don't get mail from me for a while, I could be (1) in the Soo jail for assaulting a country western signer; (2) cooking, cooking, cooking or (3) at the gym working on the marshmallows and Hershey bars. love you guys,. jojo

01.8.18   Crazy Rita

When Vangel Perroy left Albania for America, he shared the journey and a belief in opportunity with his three sons. Their quest for prosperity was ill-timed. A depression met them at their first destination, Chicago; and the jobs they found there did not survive the 1920's. Following a vague promise of work near the Canadian border of Michigan, their dreams of a new life came true in a tannery near a small town they could barely pronounce, Sault Ste. Marie. Much of the following years is now lost to dementia; however, early on, the father returned to Albania to live out his life. The eldest son, Christis, accompanied him, seeking a wife from their village. But, already the son was drifting from the old ways. He fell in love with a young girl of scant social status from a neighboring village and, ignoring his family's wishes, married her. A year later, on August 18, 1931, they had a child; and Chris Perroy, freshly American, gave his daughter a name from a song popular in his new country. He named her Rio Rita.

Immigration was a slow process then. There was money to save and a house to build for the wife and infant he had to leave behind. It would be 1939 before they could join him in Michigan. Five years from the time she was reunited with her father, Rio Rita Perroy and I became life-long friends.

An average of one hundred million tons of freight vital to the war effort steamed through the Sault Ste. Marie locks each year of World War II. The unhappy designation of primary target brought 15,000 troops to protect the St. Mary's River. There were no seasonal tourists lining the lock walls, only soldiers endlessly marching back and forth along the piers. The waterfront parks became anti-aircraft gun emplacements. The park fountain where small feet splashed in time with the Canadian pipers was off limits. And the pipers had gone to war. Under a canopy of barrage balloons for years, an entire population was so accustomed to their presence that weather became a secondary observation when looking skyward over Sault Ste. Marie. One had only to raise the eyes slightly to be reminded bombs could fall from the sky . . . as if such heavenly reminders were needed in addition to the blackout curtains, sirens, searchlights, sugarless cereal. No wonder children lined up on defense stamp day at school, hopeful that their ten cents a week would help win the war. In August, 1945 the world entered the atomic age. One month later, Rio Rita and I entered junior high school.

My seventh grade expectations were not scholastic. Leaving Garfield Elementary as tallest person in the school, I began praying in early August that my classmates would have colossal growth spurts. I would settle for even one miracle, preferably female, to stand beside me in the back row of group photos; someone my height to walk with me in school hallways, a soulmate in the search for Size Tall. All that Presbyterian Sunday School paid off. Also, God grants you special favors if, by the age of 12, you have not robbed a liquor store or misplaced your sisters. In addition to classmates elevated by Divine Grace, I received a bonus. My new tall friend, Rita, and I made the junior high cheerleading squad. We now remember that so did everyone else who signed up.

Rita had dropped the Rio from her name, but this did not dilute her uniqueness. No one would ever presume she had been born and raised within the Sault city limits. All that Balkans blood and the whispers from her childhood in Albania would forever keep her from blending into ordinary. As a young girl, she is delicately recalled as spirited and, on occasion, brash . . . early stages of the fiery, dramatic woman she would become, passionate in all things and straightforward with every living creature. The clipped and exact diction, embellished with fluent hand language and quick tilt of the chin, would always be characteristic. She could toss her head and hips at the same time as she marched down a hall and never miss a step. Her exotic looks and spectacular stride turned young boys' heads. Rita's beauty was enhanced by years; but it was her walk that became legendary. And her love story.

As if caught in its warp, Andronika Perroy remained forever on Albanian time, spurning familiarity beyond her ethnicity, refusing the English language and driving lessons. She fretted constantly over her only child. Perhaps her own poor beginnings would finally be overlooked by the Albanian community when she succeeded in raising a daughter who was educated, obedient and chaste. Rita was to be married into a respected Albanian family, and although there was no formal contract, the negotiations for her mother's social salvation had already begun. Thus, the Perroys, if not conventional, were devoted to Rita. She was exquisitely groomed, and her natural flair with clothes was indulged. But, although they loved their daughter, they restricted and controlled her with their narrow ways, denying her much of the normal teen social life and all of the early dating experience. The possibility of the family's ruination by some boy would send Andronika Perroy into tears and Olympic handwringing as her husband shouted prophesies of his early death. Hence, The Plan.

By high school, adolescent crushes were following the natural course to real boyfriends. The Albanian Wild Child and I encountered a roadblock on our paths to dating in our freshman year of high school set up by our parents and known in English and Albanian as the "boyfriend ban." We were far back in the quest for first love or at least a trophy hickey. By the next year, when I was allowed to date, Rita and I had become co-conspirators in a romantic plan that was equal parts innocence and deception. This moralistic balance, however, may have tipped in favor of our side. We deceived our parents, but we thought there was nothing wrong with our methods. Rita was occasionally allowed to spend an overnight with a female classmate who had two parents in residence known to Chris and Andronika Perroy. This was a very slim roster, but my father, mother and I made the cut. Behind my bedroom door Rita and I, at first, traded sweaters, read "real romance" magazines and experimented with eyelash curlers. We were sisters to each other before we became partners in crime. Ultimately, unknown to the Perroys, and under my parents' unwitting sponsorship, these home visits blossomed into occasions of ordinary teen activity for Rita . . . piling into a booth at Krempel's Drug Store, dancing at the Youth Center and, eventually, walking home with boys or, rather, one special boy.

Robert Sibbald seemed an unlikely football hero. Soft-spoken and courteous, his athleticism was as much presence as physique. He

was called "Duke" and moved within that male inner circle of the
favored, those marked by a mysterious singularity which did not
come strictly from athletics, looks, intellect or opportunity. But the
boy with the lithe, quiet walk was portrayed as a "vicious tackler and
blocker" a "football star" by sportswriters. He had the respect of his
coaches, the admiration of his teammates and the loyalty of friends.
Later, they would prove their devotion to him long after the football
season ended for Duke Sibbald. In a yearbook photo, he remains nice
looking, crewcut, wearing a serious expression and holding a football.
Memories of this time happen upon him in the school hallways, always
with his buddies as they traveled in a jostling pack or gathered silently
like a group of watchful tomcats near the stairwell. Even these images
of Duke in happy times are overshadowed with sadness, knowing what
he could have become. Everyone remembers he and Rita Perroy were
in love.

I don't know which threat or promise finally swayed Chris Perroy, but
at the end of her junior year, Rita won half the battle to go to the prom
with Duke Sibbald. However, there was no happy anticipation in the
Perroy household, only the escalating war for understanding between
Rita and her mother. On the night of the dance, as her friends posed
before front doors and blooming hedges, adjusting corsages and smiles
for the family cameras, Rita left the house in a borrowed dress on her
first real date. Andronika Perroy refused to come out of her bedroom
or to cease weeping. Sixty years later, nothing comes to me about that
night except an unexpected realization that the person who would take
away Duke's future and forever change so many lives drove me to my
junior prom. When the school year ended, Rita was sent to relatives in
Chicago for the summer. She was there when the phone call came.

We grow old, and our memories turn selective. As with aging eyesight,
images become indistinct if we try to study them too closely, the edges
sloughing off, leaving only particulars. And sometimes the heart, in
self-defense, chooses what we remember. If you could ask each person
who had belonged to our inmost group within the Class of '51, all
would agree that in some way each of us changed one night, although
to most the details of our common tragedy are no longer clear. Perhaps
that summer evening in 1950 began, like many others, with some
of the guys going out for a ride around town. But this time the boy

driving had been drinking, and out on the Old Pickford Road he drove his car into the back of a truck. No fatalities were listed on the official accident report, but two lives ended. Duke Sibbald, a passenger, did not walk away from the scene . . . he did not walk anywhere again or use his arms. The driver was not injured physically, but left with his own remorse and the censure of an entire town, he, too, did not recover. The alcohol which started his evening eventually ended his life.

Rita has given new meaning to powerful adjectives: vivacious, emotional, wild . . . a lovely gypsy girl we still call "Crazy Rita." When she returned to the Soo for her senior year, she was her own version of pragmatic. As if everyone had thrust some form of widowhood upon her, she was expected to play a role beyond her high school years, a charade her honesty could not accept but was unable to resent openly. Aside from her close friends, other girls misunderstood her lack of dramatic grief, and the boys all kept a respectful distance. Immediately transported from the accident to a downstate hospital, Duke would remain there long after his classmates were graduated and strewn across the fertile realm of possibilities. Rita graduated a National Thespian, member of the choir, home room vice president, school paper staffer, beloved member of the everlasting circle we now call the Soo Sisterhood. That June in 1951 she left Sault Ste. Marie behind. One afternoon a year later, as I was helping a friend push his gas-starved Beetle back to my dorm, Rio Rita Perroy put on a wedding gown, and somewhere in Chicago married the man her parents had chosen for her. Predictably, the marriage did not last forever. Everyone, including Chris Perroy, who privately thought the match unworthy of his daughter, was surprised it lasted twelve years. Shunned by the disgraced Perroy family for divorcing her husband, Rita was left to support her son and herself. She asked Estee Lauder for a job.

Estee Lauder's early marketing techniques included seeking out only the most prestigious accounts, a precedent which to this day limits sales of her products to high end department stores and boutiques. She required style and elegance in her representatives, and trained them thoroughly. Rita was soon selling for Lauder at Saks on Michigan Avenue and scenting downtown Chicago with "Estee." During the

'60's, Lauder not only went international, but also introduced her Clinique products, together with personal skin care and makeup consultations. Rita was a natural for this new venture in the cosmetic world. She had the face to inspire a thousand makeovers and the talent to work profitable magic for the company. When TWA established a grooming administrator position, she was hired as a consultant to assist with personal makeup and hairstyles for its female flight attendants.

I picked out my husband myself, and my marriage lasted twice as many years as Rita's. I also topped her birth score by three; and absolutely won out in the puppy, kitten, hamster, rabbit and piranha count over the years. Although blurred by my aforementioned selective memory and the speed at which they passed, those years, for each of us, in decidedly different ways, were our most creative. I took pleasure from thinking of Rita, flourishing, finally on her own in what I imagined to be a glamorous world with downtown apartment, exciting friends, Sasoon haircuts and silk blouses. Also, she could send me cosmetic samples to keep me presentable for those impromptu little functions at the pediatrician's office. So that I wouldn't run out of new ideas we could disagree on, articles torn from the "Tribune" with books and cassettes arrived regularly from Chicago. Eventually, there is a bittersweet triumph when the children do not need you for an entire weekend . . . fortunately for me, during a time when round trip fare to Chicago from Escanaba was less than the weekly milk bill.

We simply left the years in our dust. Rita drove a bright yellow Kharman Ghia convertible at one, breathtaking speed with top down (the better to shout at saner drivers or incredibly handsome men). Like two passengers aboard a crazed bumblebee, we sped into the city, blowing Black Cat smoke to the wind and singing every song on the Chicago stations. I was treated to concerts, theater, exhibits and blues bars. Later, there were quiet times as my friend sought to restore my courage. When couples reach the bottom of their marriage, they may need a second honeymoon, counseling or police intervention. I tried all three. As bad went to worse for me, Rita provided a safehouse, sent me money and clothes.

Shortly before our hips and knees began to send little warnings, we both slipped into the civil service pool, hoping that, buoyed by a pension, we could stay afloat through our retirement years. Rita retired from the Cook County court system; and giving up on Gucci handbags and the big city after three muggings, moved to Lower Michigan. But, she may always seem as if she is just visiting South Haven although she is faithful to her volunteer work at the art center and generous with letters to the local newspaper in support of her Libertarian views. After all these years since junior high, our friendship is without sharp edges, smoothed by the rough times we've passed through together and beautifully burnished by constant use.

Andronika Perroy is gone, and I can recall her at her best, bringing countless dishes of food to the table and urging everyone to "eat, eat, eat," then shyly excusing herself from conversation with nervous little gestures which always involved her ever-present apron. She liked me, I think. I know that she was the only person who always thought I was too thin. For this, and seeing her differently now through my woman's eyes, I liked her, too. The once robust and unrestrained Chris Perroy passed away in a nursing facility tended faithfully by the daughter he had loved and tried ineffectually to champion, but could not remember. Rita and I have moved up the chain to assume the responsibility of enforcing wisdom upon our children and their children.

Crazy Rita and I are planning a trip together. We have abandoned our earlier dreams of dancing with Greek sailors on Santorini, but we have not given up on the barge trip through France, relishing the countryside and cuisine. And, of course, the wine . . . much like ourselves . . . mature, rare, a little mysterious and definitely not too sweet.

01.8.28   Maggie and An Invitation From Dexter

I have Maggie for a "houseguest" while Po's youngest, Todd, completes a term at Northern. He stopped by one evening on his way to Marquette from the Soo, and after the usual small talk, asked me if I missed Maggie. I did miss the dear old dog. For months she was a comforting presence, refusing to be kept from Po's bedside. "Yes, I do miss her. How is she?" "She's in the car," he said. So, that is how I came to have an elder Golden Retriever for a temporary roommate.

Maggie and I made a trip to the Soo the past weekend. She visited with family and checked out all the neighborhood garbage cans. As happy as that animal and I are together, there were some uncomfortable moments riding with her in the car. Maggie can violate every section of the Clean Air Act by just being around, not to mention those moments enhanced by her Alpo gas. No amount of bathing with Herbal Essence seems to help. So, upon our return, I took her to the vet, who earned his fee by checking all of Maggie's orifices and ventured a guess that it was her thyroid. Pray we don't ever have thyroid trouble!! Maggs is now on medication and my Honda, too, is recovering on a regimen of air freshener. Love from jojo, anniecat and Maggie

01.8.29

Dear Jo,

I was certainly happy to finally find you at home having suspected that you were still searching for Maggie. Maybe Pat Norton would have to do a painting of you chasing through neighborhoods in the Soo on a trail of empty garbage cans.

We received your last email as we were walking out the door to leave for a week in our "Beach Condo" half way between Pawley's Island and Murrell's Inlet. This condo is very similar to our condo which also follows us to the Mountains and to Michigan. Wish you were pulling in next door. This is the Grand Strand and has to be the best beach left on the Southeast coast. Beautiful! When we read your letter, we immediately thought of an idea which

you can try on for a day or two and see if it
fits. How about a few weeks visit at our house
and we take a trip for part of it while you
enjoy Beaufort and area your own way: you can
have a Kayak here in Battery Creek and go all
the way to Africa or it is a 20 minute drive
to the beach. We might like to leave Dexter
with you as it would be Earl's dream to get
away from him for a few days. He would not tie
you down for trips out of town as his kennel
is two blocks from the house. The down side is
that I would not be here to spend time with you
which I was looking forward to. I am thinking
we could plan some time before and after our
trip. Mull all this over.

Love, Mothagoose and the Old Fellow

01.8.30   RoadTrekkie

Burba, Please do plan a trip this winter. I will be delighted to look
after the house and Dexter Dog. Earl has sold me on RoadTrek
motorhomes. I hope the new brochures from their factory arrive
soon. The picture of the guy with (golf) balls is showing some wear;
likewise the page which illustrates how I should shower in the aisle
(while stirring beans on the stove) and the list of options Earl wanted
me to memorize. I'm already planning my "Trekky" wardrobe . . . mix
and match waddable attire which will store easily in one wheel well,
and unstylish enough so as not to attract the old guys illustrated on
page 6. You may be skeptical, but just wait until I pull in next to you
in my 190-Versatile, and begin to zip on my Florida room (optional)
with PRIVACY PANELS. What do you do in a zip-on Florida room
which requires privacy panels????? Is this something about rving that
I should know? I have sent friends to Wisconsin this weekend to buy
powerball tickets for me. If I win the $120 million, I am going for
the Model 200, baby. I will pay off the Pope and an old boyfriend's

alimony, then kidnap him to drive cross-country with me. (Is this when I use the privacy panels?)

Scott will spend another week with us before he has to return to Ft. Lauderdale. We have had fun! Spent an afternoon at the U.P. State Fair in Escanaba. Ate corn dogs, elephant ears, chili fries, mylanta tablets; and then went into the birthing tent which Scott was happy to learn was showing no activity. I wanted to have my "Photo Taken With The Big Cats" for $15, but Scott claims they don't make film with speed fast enough to capture me going in and out of the tiger cage. Jojo

1.9.2   The Sparkles Incident

Last week our neighbors' cat, Sparkles, was attacked and badly injured; and rounding up the usual suspects meant coming to complain to me about my wild little anniecat. I'm happy to write that annie has been thoroughly exonerated of the Sparkles incident. My neighbor called yesterday to report the culprit cat, a large yellow stray, had returned and broken poor Sparkles' leg this time. So the cat hunt is on here at Squaw Point. Am keeping anniecat in the house for a few days or until the armed Special Crimes Unit solves this case. love from jojo, annieiwasframedcat and Maggie

01.9.21   God Save America

Burba and Earl, I think we have all fallen into this state of shock and worry. The President is still contacting certain foreign governments, aiming to build a coalition before anyone proceeds. We read into the briefings that this will lead to something more than random air strikes . . . it will be some sort of sustained conflict. The reality of war is bad enough, but we have these faceless enemies who hide out in little ranch style houses all over our country. They slither in and out of international airports daily, their cells multiply all over the world like a cancer. Our intelligence has egg on its face because we have relied too much on technology in lieu of good old sneaky, mobile, thinking, drinking (Bushmill's) SPIES. I agree with you that indiscriminate hate and retaliation are bad things; but I have this constant hope that those responsible for the death and destruction here will be found and punished without more loss of innocents. The past two weeks have gradually evolved to an uneasy normalcy. It is truly a time of grieving. Everything seems so quiet and sad. There are no happy sounds anywhere. Even the woods and beach were a bit ugly . . . cold, drizzling rain and unrelenting NE wind. Tilly gave up walking with me for a while. Dogs don't appreciate the relief of exercise or the invigoration of fresh air. It is the only relief I feel. God Save America.

Hi Jo, This has been a difficult week. Our new RV arrived in the middle of the war disaster. So we laughed and cried and were nervous about the DC branch of the family. Don's status is definitely up in the air. Pam and the children are to get in the car and head south if any additional worries come

up. We hauled our sorrow and dismay with us to Columbia to take delivery of the Kountry Star. It is fab. However, the most fun we had was hanging out in the Roadtreks and making plans for you. We like the 190 Popular. Earl was ecstatic to see that you could cook and shower at the same time. I will try to write more when my mind is in better condition. Love, Barbara

01.9.27   Remembering Einstein

In early fall, I often think of the first days here on Squaw Point, and my heart remembers the special friend who shared them with me. This is his story.

1998.10.27 My neighbors have retired and moved to southern Wisconsin. Their children have grown and scattered, leaving only the family dog to complain about this upheaval and the fact that at least one Wisconsin condo community discriminates against dogs. Of all the friends and family who voiced concern for that great old dog, apparently I was the only one who also volunteered to care for him until a son and his family completed their new home and could claim him. This was no big deal because it only meant he would now be staying overnight, having already moved to my back porch for his golden years. I have also had his company in the garden, on the beach and during long walks down the road. He cheerfully prances along, acknowledging my comments, praise, laughter, admonitions and tears with the same soft eyes and generous sweep of tail.

Would you believe someone who failed most efforts with math would end up living with A. Einstein, and that he was alive and well as half Great Pyrenees and half Golden Retriever? Einstein has filled my heart at the same rate he depletes the store of X-Large Milk Bones. He will be ten next birthday, and is unforgiving about meal schedules, naps and bedtimes; yet, when Po asked for help, he squeezed into the back seat of my car and traveled to the Soo with me. There he spent time tethered without complaint, sensing the sadness that had come to her house.

My neighbor's son drove over from Green Bay last weekend to tell me he will come for Einstein on November first. He had moved his family to a more rural area where big dogs can run free. His little girls were with him, and fell all over their old friend. Einstein was beyond pure joy at seeing them.

All this brings me to Halloween. I'm invited to a costume party, and plan to celebrate with my pal Einstein. I will dress as Orphan Annie and will be accompanied by you-know-who in a clever disguise as dog Sandy. It will be a night to remember, don't you agree? Next week the garden and beach will be as empty as the back porch . . . and the road will seem longer.

01.10.1   Carrot Cuticles

Hi Jo,

Received my Burt's Bees care package and was delighted. Send invoice. I know those products were expensive, although they can be eaten during a hurricane which makes me want to keep my Carrot Cuticle Remover ever handy. I dreamed about you and your old boyfriend last night. You were wearing his Soo Hi letter sweater over your good dress and it is not a 'look' that is highly recommended for us Grands. We have so many plans for February that we can hardly wait for you to get here. Is it almost February? I keep seeing you in Off White, old boyfriend leaning jauntily on his walker, me standing by your side

in Assorted Vegetables. Love, bjl

01.10.2   Colds and Crusades

Just a note to advise that I have won my battle against the common cold, which a few days ago seemed uncommonly vicious and life threatening. A strain which attacks people who brag about avoiding a cold for two years. By last Tuesday I realized I was sick of orange juice and that my flannel jammies were looking too lived in. anniecat, who was devoted through the first hours of my crisis, tired of my moping around. She ended her vigil on my lap to take up chasing the bottle caps and toast crusts which littered the floor around my chair. Since I slept through much of the sniper disaster on television, I could use my periods of consciousness to finish reading Lent's "In The Fall." As my luck would have it, I recovered in time to keep my dentist appointment.

Am waiting for the pumpkin bars to cool before I drown them in cream cheese frosting. I have to bring something for the coffee hour tomorrow after church, and thought the pumpkin would be suitably seasonal and all that frosting would help my contribution pass for Lutheran. Seems as if this is the time of year we Yoopers drag our feet . . . too early for deer season. I'll soon begin my treks up the bleachers as Abby starts this year for Escanaba basketball; Kyle and Eric for Rapid River. Molly has taken up competitive cheerleading, whatever that is, in addition to helping organize some group "teens for proper choices" or something sounding like that. Although I don't think this group is entirely food-driven, she is pleased with her part in supporting a salad bar and "make your own" sub sandwich table as part of the lunch program She is just a freshman . . . imagine the crusades she will launch in 3-1/2 more years. I must take very good care of myself to ensure being around to see what Molly does with her life. Love, jojo and annieRNcat

01.10.13   RV Cult and Pickford

Hooray! You really are out there somewhere. I thought you and Earl had joined some sort of RV cult and cut all ties with your more secular friends who still drive sedans. Is the new "wheeler" as great as I imagine? At least you don't water whatever is cooking while you shower. Made a quick trip to Pickford area this week. My Aunt Sara Sawyers died at the age of 95. She was the last of my aunties, and has joined Uncle Clive; my grandparents, Ephriam and Susan McKee Sawyers; Aunt Reta Sawyers Hart McDonald and Uncle Cal Hart; my parents, Eddie and Elva Sawyers Rust; Marlow Ladd and my dear sister Patricia Rust Veum Ladd, leaving another name on the mother earth near Pickford. I will write more later about my travel plans and my increasing popularity as a hostess since my Roadtrek film arrived. That tour of the Ontario plant entertains everyone. love, jo

01.10.14   Aunt Sara

Aunt Sara (Rye) Sawyers died at the age of 95. She was the last of my aunties, the wife of my mother's brother, Clive Sawyers. She and Clive owned a large farm near Pickford (30 miles from the Soo). This was a real working farm of that era. The huge barn (with haylofts for jumping out of!) housed long lines of cows, a large pen of pigs, a henhouse, grainery and two pair of the finest and largest draft horses in the Upper Peninsula. Surrounding the farmhouse and barn, immense hayfields offered a drivers' education site for my cousins as well as the season's crops.

Our family gathered at the farm for many holidays, my grandparents Sawyers at the ends of the "big" table, surrounded by my aunts and uncles and older cousins. The younger cousins all sat at the kitchen table, which wasn't too bad a deal because as soon as you moved up to the big table you had to help with preparations and washing up after the meal. I was the cousin who always wanted to spend time at the farm during the summer with my cousins, Gayle, Marjean and Vern, so have happy memories of those summer haying days. The "threshers" came during one of my visits. These men moved from farm to farm with the threshing machine, helping one another bring in their crops. I believe it was a somewhat "social" event which involved hard labor. When the threshers came, Aunt Sara, Gayle and Marjean began each day at dawn, baking and cooking until the pantry table was filled with pies and bread, and great pans of side pork and potatoes fried on the stove to feed them.

In addition to being a farm wife, Aunt Sara was a schoolteacher. She taught a one-room school until she was (I think) nearly 60, at which time the school system changed, and so did the requirements for teaching . . . so she went back to school at that tender age to earn her degree and certificate so that she could continue her teaching.

Meanwhile, she played the organ in the Donaldson Presbyterian Church every Sunday until she was well into her 80's. She played the piano beautifully; and, as a little girl, I was so happy when I could sit on the piano bench with her while she played my favorite "Falling Waters" in the front room of the farmhouse. She wore Helena Rubenstein's Apple Blossom perfume, and always carried that scent, even when she came from the milk house or the far reaches of the barn.

As I wrote, she is the last of my aunties, and was buried Wednesday near Pickford next to Uncle Clive and close to my grandparents, Ephriam and Susan Elizabeth McKee Sawyers; Aunt Reta (who was really Mayme Margreta, but didn't like that name so shortened it) and Uncle Cal (whence Scott Calvin Beggs); my parents and my sister, Po. Leaving the funeral, Marjean asked me to take Sara's brother's wife with me in my car, and what a wonderful experience that was . . . all the way out to the cemetery and back along the familiar roads. She told me stories and pointed out all the houses along the way and told me who had lived there and how we were related, bringing back many memories and names I hadn't heard since my mother, Gramma the Great, died.

And, of course, there was the funeral meal at the Bruce Township Hall which included covered dishes, trays, pans filled with the finest cooking anywhere. I once again sat at the "big table" with all my cousins. So many of my family now missing from that long ago table at the farm. However, it was a good time to catch up on each other and grandchildren, sharing time together. Aunt Sara surely must have liked that part of her sendoff best . . . better than the funeral service where she was praised for the accomplishments she was modest about and which included yet another Presbyterian sermon.

01.11.1   Halloween and Working Girl

Burba. The trick or treaters will be out tonight, and once again I have stocked up on my favorite candy. The turnout here on my road is very disappointing—perhaps one or two vans will pull up in my drive and leave off a load of little revelers, but that's about it. And then I must eat all the leftover candy. After all those bite-sized Paydays, I probably won't even go to bed tonight, just sit up and watch reruns of news briefings and wait for the world series to begin. Besides, if I fall asleep these days, I have romantic dreams of Donald Rumsfeld.

We had snow yesterday . . . wet, clumpy, stinging, globs of it. No beautiful, "fluffy blanket covering the world with white," it blew in here from the northwest in gusts of 50 mph plastering the remaining leaves to the lakeside windows, turning the whole county to slop and killing two people on the highways. If I only had my Roadtrek, I would be halfway to Kentucky by now or at least out of the range of the latest snowmobile commercials imploring me to "Think Snow." Your neighborhood must be changed these days with the navy pilots on alert. I think of them and picture their children's little hot wheel toys on the sidewalks of the cul de sac near you. I recall how everyone in Battery Creek called them "our boys."

I start at the meat plant in a couple of weeks, wrapping venison through deer season. I will work at the law office some in December allowing the secretaries to each take time off. The portrait group called me again to model. I will wear a black hat and . . . Yes, Earl! . . . a dress, as well. Looks as if Ensign Twp. will have their taxes for my property again this year. Am off for my walk down the road. Many bowhunters in the woods, so I wear my multi-colored jacket these days and hope that some hunter doesn't mistake me for a deer with fashion sense. love from jojo and anniecat

Jo, We arrived home and enjoyed finding a letter from you. We had been off in the Okephenokee Swamp on the Swanee River (Far, Far Away). It was beautiful! The Georgia Campgrounds are the best and only outdone by Alabama, so we went to three of them. We were also joined over one weekend by friends who toured with us on Jekyll Island. We took a boat tour in the Swamp and learned much about it. Next time, we will rent a boat or canoe and tour alone. Lots of alligators—did you know in

The Book of Job that the Lord declared them King of the Beasts? Since I have been reading the Bible, I am a fount of that sort of information. Speaking of reading, we have both recently read "The Voyage" and will give it to you for Beaufort reading. No Jo, it is NOT the story about the woman who drove her Roadtrek into the Mississippi and later on enjoyed floating into New Orleans.

When you have sex dreams of Donald Rumsfeld, do you call him Mr. Secretary or do you call him Don? Do not try to tell me you call him Rumsie. Well, Jo, here we go again. I kind of have a thing for him. too. He is the only one that doesn't cause me to turn off CNN and watch the weather channel through three hours of ironing. I get very distressed at the constant poking and criticizing of the Government. That Paula gives me a BIG pain. I don't think she gets to interview Rumsie. We did not have a vacation from the news during our travels because the great State of Georgia provides cable to its campers. Guys sit around in tents and watch Monday Night Football. And, wasn't it a relief that the Pack did not play this week?

Boy, are you ever busy working. Do not get your employment mixed up and arrive at the meat plant wearing only a hat. You'd be frozen buns. Sorry about the snow; it is 79 here this morning. Love, from Momma and Poppa Goose and poor, pitiful Dexter.

01.12.1   Preparing for Christmas 2001, Maggie and the Meat Plant

Burba, I continue replacing Christmas lights in the window boxes. The bulbs appear to be wired to an unseen timer which kills off the very string that is most tightly wound around the pine boughs. Each death is set for exactly 3 minutes after you have finished the job and are hauling your cold old bones back to shelter. With winter whistling across Bay de Noc ice from the north, the wind chill dropped to—25 degrees. Not even the Bishop's planned annual appearance at our little church nor the promise of Pearl Larson's banana bread at coffee hour could pry many of the Stonington Lutherans from the comfort of their woodstoves. All those raffle tickets and bake sales for a new furnace at the church seemed questionable effort yesterday upon realizing we had a fair weather congregation. One would expect a hardier lot when names end with " . . . . sen" or " . . . son!"

I finished up my seasonal gig helping process venison at Michigan Meats. Three weeks of 10 hour days when the hunt is at peak. Each deer that comes in is recorded, and instructions for its packaging follow it past the skinners to the butchers and, finally, to the wrappers. A surprising number of choices are made before the venison finds a final resting place in the hunter's home freezer. In addition to the routine choice of portions per package, customers now can select from a variety of sausage, lunch meat and bacon prepared from their deer. My dad, who spent most of his working life as a meat cutter, would have been amused to see me in a butcher's apron. I make new friends in my employers' wonderful family (even the grandchildren work during the season), and hear countless hunting stories. I go from the freezers and smokers at Michigan Meats to my old desk at the law office where I will fill in for a day here and there. The desk job allows me to be with my old friends, keep my mind from getting any soggier, and guarantees my invitation to the office Christmas party.

So, here I am summoning up the Christmas spirit in the time allotted to get a tree into the house, wrap gifts for those who didn't fall for my "Wouldn't you rather have cash to shop at Old Navy?" ploy, buy some cookies and watch the Charlie Brown Christmas Special. My tree is MUCH SMALLER this year. I found the tree merchants haven't heard the threats of recession.

This shrinking tree thing could be good. Last year I brought in a spruce larger than the Downtown Gladstone Tree at City Hall and had to tie a rope around the top and over one of the log beams in the ceiling to raise it upright into the tree stand. I am making my temporary houseguest, dear Maggie, a polar fleece coat to cover the parts of her old back where the hair doesn't grow anymore. I assured Todd it would be of tasteful design. I even took a Talbots label from one of Po's old coats to sew on the collar. Maggs will go back to the Soo next week to live out her days. I will miss her greatly . . . . but don't tell Todd because he may bring her back. Love and Merry Christmas from jojo, anniecat and Maggie

01.12.13   Irish Walking Cape

B, I, drove to Marquette in a sleet storm on Friday to shop the sales. Having completed my Christmas shopping at 20% off and visiting with sister Sandy, I continued on to Houghton Saturday a.m. to visit with Dave and attend the Moscow Ballet performance Saturday night with some friends from . . . . Moscow. The Moscow Ballet is a very young company, but classical and gifted; and I enjoyed Irina and friends (when I could understand them). Looking ahead, the big printing on my calendar is for Molly's piano recital, Abby's gymnastics meet, Amy's band concert and Ryan's hockey game . . . Sometime between Letterman's monologue and Rumsie's news conference, I will sleep.

The UPS man stopped by the other day and delivered a lovely blue gift box from Scott. OhOh! The sender didn't seal it with scotch tape and staple the edges and tie the ribbon in a knot to foil curious old ladies who love to get packages and know they are supposed to wait until Christmas to open them. I thought I had better take a peek to make sure nothing was damaged in shipping. Wouldn't you? And so this explains why I am writing to you while wearing this most beautiful garnet cashmere Irish Walking Cape; and forgive me for admitting that I keep walking by the mirror to see if I am still changed into one of the heroines from my favorite old books. Do they wear walking capes in Beaufort on cool evenings? I hope so, because I plan to never be without this truly beautiful and magical garment. Move over ladies wearing swampers and sad quilted jackets in Elmer's Market, I am moving through the produce section as Rebecca de Wynter. Attention KMart shoppers! Scarlet O'Hara seen in Health and Beauty Aids. Hope all is well with you, and you are wrapping as you purchase, saving the receipts and following Martha through her preparations on CBS.

HoHo from jojo and annieChristmascat

02.1.13   Packer Halter Top

Earl and Barb, Here in Florida there is nothing like watching football as the temperature hits 77 degrees out on the balcony where the brats are grilling. The last quarter was so exciting I spilled rum punch on my Packer halter top. Earlier, I had to take the 4 off the left soft cup because Scott's friends may have mistaken it for my bra size or IQ. I was delighted to see Ft. Lauderdale. I arrived on a flight from Detroit with a load of older tourist types and immigrating snowbirds in resort wear who, as one, screamed "OH NO" when the pilot announced the temperature in Lauderdale was 43 degrees that morning. This caused the secret sky marshal to leap from his seat and blow cover. Right now Scott is making more Cuban chip dip for everyone, and I'm out of punch. Love from jojo, Scott and Jackson the Rescued Greyhound

02.1.20   Amtrak Arrival

Hello Beaufort. Scott brought me a laptop, and I can now quash those rumors that I ran off with a Parrothead in a '74 Dodge Dart after the Jimmy Buffet concert. I will arrive at an Amtrak station somewhere near you about 12 hours after I leave Ft. Lauderdale. I will be the one on the platform looking like "Modern Maturity," wearing my shirt from the Buffet concert. Thank you for planning out my stay so thoughtfully. I know I will feel at home in such beautiful environs and will have Dear Dexter for company while you enjoy your trip. All I need is his schedule, a few notes re the house, your cell number and a menu for Thai takeout. Also, before you leave, we could stand on the front porch and you can point out where to find high ground. Scott's staff at North Park treated me to a limo and lunch with them before I left. I felt special, mostly because they all made it a point to say something nice about Scott. Soon. Jojo

02.3.15   Kitty Litter

Burba, Here I am in the "computer" designated corner of the garage, dislodging ice from the keyboard. Was a quick trip out here because all of Stonington is covered with a sheet of ice. Once I began the slide off the porch, there was no stopping until I met the garage door. Consequently, I have added a new twist to preparing for guests arriving during these conditions. I have filled some of the grandkids' sandpails with (clean!) kitty litter and left them out by my mailbox. I then called everyone and told them to pick up their little bucket and proceed down the driveway which, incidently, looks as if I had been driving a Zamboni instead of a Honda. Then, when they get out of the car, they are to sprinkle little handfuls of litter along their path until they find clear sidewalk. Hoping this will keep me from having fractured friends and lawsuits. Is this a good idea to pass along to Martha? She would have clever ideas for decorating the pails. Don't look for this in her "Southern Life" edition. Good to hear Earl has recovered, and will be out caring for the neighborhood again soon. Be thankful for good recoveries and that you don't have to walk around in kitty litter. Jojo

02.3.27   The Red Army Chorus and Farewell to Maggie

Burba, I'm typing this letter in the garage "office" sans heat while anniecat implores me to turn up the thermostat. The garage furnace quit while I was in Houghton for the weekend. I did make it to Dave's door before the storm hit, but we drove to and from the concert in a blizzard. What a welcome for The Red Army Chorus, some of its members perhaps coming from Siberia to perform! Each part of the program was memorable. First time I have been to an event where everyone cheered EACH number. For their final encore they sang "God Bless America" in sturdy English as everyone stood and sang along with them. One great moment to remember if we ever have another cold war. I won't be going to the Soo tomorrow to help with arrangements for Maggie. She died while I was in Houghton. Todd handling it quite well, saying he thought of having a nice obit put in the "Sault Evening News" and is planning a wake of sorts at the Downtowner Bar. I told him I felt Maggs was just holding on these past two years to make sure Todd had his feet under him before she left him on his own.

Will make this short as the ice crystals are making their way up toward my wrist . . . But, thank you for distributing the photos I collected in your neighborhood. I have nice memories when I look at my copies. Also, Earl should know that "Sunbirds" was all he said it was. I enjoyed it greatly, especially since Dave and I read the last accounts of Opet to each other in that frigid old bedroom in the farmhouse, under a mound of quilts, in the howling snowstorm, munching on a Dixie cup full of leftover Christmas M & M's. jojo and anniefrostycat

```
Jo,  I   read   the   first   sexual   chapters   of
"Prodigal  Summer"  and   then   ate  the  chocolate
brownies   frozen.   Is   there   anything   else   I
should  know  about?  Should  I  call  your  Cousin
Gayle  who  told  you  the  facts  of  life??
And . . . . If  those  Coyotes  in  the  book  are
going  to  get  killed,  tell  me  right  now  so  I
won't  read  another  page.  I  was  a  great  observer
of  them  in  DeTour.  The  scene  was  to  view  them
trouping  across  the  ice  to  Drummond  Island.
BofBB
```

02.4.18   The Flood

Greetings from the Upper Peninsula Floodplains. If you were watching national news . . . you may have caught the small story about the National Guard being called out to the U.P. This made an almost pleasant break in the daily recitation of greater disasters in other parts of the world. The tons of snow we have had were still on the ground when unusually warm weather hit, swelling the spring runoffs. With great quantities of water coursing across roads, whole areas are isolated. Wakefield, for one, is totally inaccessible tonight, and most homes have four feet of water wall to wall. This is mostly from Sunday Lake, that beautiful, rambling stretch of water which is the scene of the hydroplane Nationals and some of Todd's most triumphant or frustrating moments. This is to assure you that anniecat and I are high and dry here on Squaw Point, although the river running through Rapid River, which strangely enough is not called the Rapid River, is at flood stage. Perhaps I will have to drive in the opposite direction to Manistique for bread and Bud Lite, but not until the tornado watch for all of Delta County is lifted. That includes us. jojo and anniepussinbootscat

02.4.25   Francophiles and Firetraps

Steve and Claudia,

What a delight to read such pleasant and interesting news from overseas!!! I try to limit watching CNN and FOX to occasional timid peeks. Does anyone over there like us anymore???

The geese have quit circling in confusion, and have come home to Squaw Point. Hopefully, most of this flock will move on down the beach. This morning we have three swans gliding along in the shallows, dodging the last of the larger fragments of ice. Wish they could stay around, but they are wise to find safer waters. Their particular species has been classified a nuisance by the state; and the DNR is charged with the rather noxious duty of "keeping their numbers under control."

I made a little concert trip last weekend to Houghton to hear the St. Paul Chamber Orchestra and look in on the Dollar Bay kids. Very heavy program (Stravinski), but the orchestra was top notch . . . a really large number of musicians for a "chamber" group. A precise and graceful young woman conducted . . . . (wearing this gorgeous black crepe pantsuit which seemed to flow with the music.) The kids are busy with their new family room project . . . Pam is brushing 3 coats of finish on each aspen board before it is put on the walls. Tom is installing a gas fireplace. The whole project is beautiful. They are like two little birds constantly feathering their nest. Our calmly beautiful little Kellee was in a skip rope contest.

I will be hauling topsoil next week to repair the damage left by the welldiggers, hoping to create some semblance of a "lawn" . . . I would like to put the effort into my garden, but my neighbors are thinking I've sold out to some film studio needing a scene of devastation. The

Stonington uprising is over. Those who did not want a new community building won in a landslide township election 103 to 62. The rural mailboxes on County Road 513 are once again limited to delivery of communications approved by the U.S. Postal Service. Some families, split down the middle by the proposed millage, have reconciled; and one little old gal, a strong opponent of any change in the landscape, especially if it appears on the tax rolls, has taken the FOR SALE sign off her farm. We will keep the old grange hall, an historic firetrap, inaccessible to the handicapped and feeble, the favored gathering place for family reunions, receptions, all manner of township activity. Living just over the line, I could not vote for that township, but was close enough to the shouting to be affected by the surprising rift between the two sides. This has given me new insight into the Middle East conflict . . . and reasonable cause for pessimism. (Note: shortly after this letter, the old grange hall did indeed burn down, thankfully! while it was vacant, and has been replaced by a fine new township hall). jojo and anniecat

02.4.25   Holding On

Hi Burba, I am imagining you on the porch sipping cool refreshments as I write this wearing (yet!) my winter-weary parka. Just came in from trying to prune up some raspberry bushes, but the wind was so fierce that I had to hang on to last year's dead hollyhocks, so I have trudged back to the garage for shelter. Had a whole flock of Canada geese on the shore this morning, and all that honking sounded a lot like *"I told you it was too soon to leave the South . . . what the honk are we doing on this ice . . . . Sure, sure it sounded romantic mating over the northern marshes, but I think my little goose place is iced over. What are these strange bumps covering our flesh?"*

Are you really going to the gym 5 days a week??!!!! You will be so sculpted. You will then wear oil on your body at all times, buy embroidered undies with "Monday, Tuesday, etc.", wear glitter on your eyelids . . . white after Labor Day. As for me, I've cancelled my haircut again. It's as if the snow gods hear me making the appointment and schedule a blizzard for that day. love, jojo and anniecat

02.5.3   Prom Princess

BBofB, I spent Saturday in town helping the "Prom Princess" prepare for her first prom. This is Jeff and Laurie's Abbygail Elizabeth (I lovingly call Princess), who plans to go to med school, if she doesn't fracture her hands horribly playing basketball, softball for the high school team as a freshman, or if she succeeds in talking Jeff into letting her play hockey next year. She was like an old-fashioned prom picture . . . all net and sparkles. Her boyfriend was tall, dark and handsome, and he and gramma both had tears in our eyes when Abby came down the stairs. (I think his came from different emotions we don't even think about in front of Jeff and Laurie) Jeff did look like he was going to take off running after the car when they drove away. She called me next morning to say it was all "dreamy" (they actually say that yet??) and to thank me for being there . . . which is typically Abby. Actually, we were ALL there. Pictures included Abby; Abby & Boyfriend;; Abby, Boyfriend and Molly; Abby, Mom and Dad; Abby, Boyfriend, Mom and Dad; Grandparents Hirn; ALL of Abby's girlfriends and teammates who were not going to the dance plus some that were, and the two family Labradors. Did it happen like this for us? I seem to remember taking a bath, taking the pincurls out of hair, trying out an eyelash curler and worrying whether my Dad would really have to give us a ride to the dance. I like to think perhaps my date's eyes, too, did look a little misty when I came down the stairs.

To further share my heart with you, our sweet and loving AmyJo called last night to tell me about her first real job at the ice cream shop in their neighborhood. I told her how both Aunties Po and Sandy worked for the Soo Creamery dishing up ice cream as their first jobs. Her brother, Ryan, my Fast Puppy, is off to a good start at Bay College, managing good grades and his job at an engineered machine products company with his eye on Northern Michigan University in another year.

Apparently you found the stash of chocolate chips I left in your cupboard. If you buy some raisins, you can eat them together and say it's trail mix. Miss you, dear friends. jojo

02.6.10   Flies and Fishermen

Burba, How was the move??? I have the number of "Two Guys and a Truck," acquired sometime after Jeff and Laurie's fifth move in their early years. All this backbreaking hauling could arguably mean that if we sue our children for disability benefits, we wouldn't have to bequeath them any of our assets. This is a good thought. I will mention this to my friends in the attorneys' office. Could be legal precedence. I have finished most of the yard work . . . ill-timed about two days post giant mosquito invasion of the U.P. Terrible this year. Perhaps the short season of warm weather we will have has inspired them to frantic hatch, bite, mate, die cycle. Something similar to the Yooper life. But all is blooming outside my screen door . . . appreciated even more intensely because of the delay. Huge lilacs . . . and my cherry tree is covered with blossoms and ruby throated hummingbirds. The eagles have returned to the sand spit out front, and anniecat spends a lot of time napping in safety behind my sofa. Dave was here for the weekend and we got a whole day of fishing in Saturday. It began to rain about noon, but we stayed out there . . . was just so much fun sharing that small space between port and starboard, devouring soggy ham sandwiches and talking the day away in that subdued tone that fishermen unconsciously adopt when the motor is shut down. love you, jojo and anniecowardlycat

02.6.29   Demolition

Beautiful Burba of Beaufort: Jeff and Laurie are gutting the entire second floor of their home. This involves face masks, large dumpsters and chutes from the upstairs windows. I am cooking today to bring in a meal for everyone on the demolition crew. This was the contribution they preferred from me. Everyone turned down my offer to hang around with a crowbar. But, I have removed one of the old doors off the lake side of my house alone to hurry things along for the carpenter who hasn't kept his word yet about showing up this "spring." Am sure that some day when I am sweated up and covered with grime, smelling of smoke from the brush pile, our friend MaryEllen will appear again, probably in a newer pink outfit, bearing a bottle of chilled Pinot waving photos of a recent getaway which included a petal-strewn hot tub.

Many plans are made for the 4th of July. Rapid River's parade stops traffic going through town on US-2 while the freshly washed logging trucks, farm equipment and emergency vehicles creep by throngs of admirers lined up each side of Main Street. Sirens blaring and lights flashing, an uninterrupted stream of Yooper automotive glitz passes the cheering crowd as "souped up" lawn tractors weave in and out of the procession. Softball games, pony rides, queen contest will follow, but we head back to the water to watch the sail races which pass our beach on a course to the head of the bay. The jetskis and pedalboat launched, the day is finished in the water . . . swimming, tubing or just sitting in the old aluminum lawn chairs with feet in the warm shallows, heads lifted to the waterwind and July sun. When the day is ending, we can watch the fireworks from Gladstone and Escanaba light up the sky over the bay as we throw another log on the bonfire and memorize each dear, firelit face on a happy 4th of July . . .

It is now Saturday, and I am finally finishing this after returning from the demolition site. I have no words for it . . . . so will take my dust covered empty casserole dishes into the house and shower off the leftover particles of tile from the kids' old bathroom. Boy, I could sure use a hot tub with flower petals! love, jojo and anniedemocat

02.8.11   Earl Saves the Economy

Dear jojo,

As the stock market prepared to go into crash mode, Earl started a program of money spending. The results of which are easily seen in the market rise. First, he decided that he wanted to replace all the stair steps, front and back, with new wood and repaint EVERYTHING closely attached. Then a new sidewalk in decking style

JOAN RUST

was added to the water side of the house. He
is building a train room and planning a very
expensive model RR for the basement (train
warranted to crash as often as Amtrak). He
is building two wonderful model ships for his
buddies. He is getting some new teeth which
will take care of the dentist's car payments
forever. Yesterday afternoon it was 105. Jo,
the metal tools get so hot if they were laid
in the sun that you had to pick them up with
gloves. The crowbar for removing the old steps,
had to have water run on it after lunch to get
it back to a usable state. Thank goodness it is
humid because I can think how good it must all
be for my skin. We drink the well dry everyday.
Two good books from the Library. "The Blue
Bird House" by Rae Ellen Lee and "Lost Nation"
by Jeffrey Lent. The last one is so powerful
that I am reading it in small doses followed
by Northern Living and Cooking Heavy! How is
Todd doing with the insurance business? Tell
him that I think it is absolutely necessary for
him to move close to the agency and close to
a church. The house should have large windows
so the citizens can view his evening prayer
meetings. Barb

02.9.5   Traveling to Taos

We had our final meeting to plan the First Annual Stonington Family
Fun Night . . . which will be staged Saturday at the community park
across from the store. The committees have planned acts on the stage
(a flatbed trailer) including the three Olson sisters singing; Hertha
Wicklund playing the harmonica; the Petersons on keyboard and
singing; as well as "The Doily Sisters", a local comedy act; and Hank
Bosworth on the accordian. There will be a style show of "clever
costuming", including a bride who is actually our layminister, Sam.

Needless to say, he is the only man in Stonington above question who would do this. Corn roast, potluck supper, bingo tent, hayrides on Clickners haywagon, facepainting, games and pony rides for the children. Later, a bonfire and singalong. Our committee plans an afterglow which will be brought on by toasting ourselves with large quantities of Bud Lite. Am excited about your trip to Ireland. I hear there is a ferry that runs from Wales to the Isle and is 7 stories tall and everyone parties and dances the entire trip. It sounds as if they do a lot of that in Ireland even when they aren't crossing on ferries.

Daughter Kim and I only traveled as far as Taos. We did it all: drove down through Eagle Eye in a hailstorm, visited the pueblos, ALL the galleries, ate the *green* chili, then drove back up to Denver with a Martin Linville painting tucked behind the camping gear. Photos and documentary will be presented at a future date. Every mother should have at least one such journey with her daughter . . . together experiencing new places, ordering unfamiliar food at unlikely hours, and being roommates. Isn't it as if we seem to drop our guard and the heart softens while sharing those last moments before sleep comes? We hope to be with our daughters when needed. It is intensely splendid to be together just for the fun of it. jojo and anniecat

02.10.1   Drowning the Dessert

Burba, Recovering this a.m. from a two-party progressive dinner Darlene and I put on last night. She and John are spending a long weekend at their "camp", so we thought this would be a fun way to do some entertaining together since their place is only a few miles from mine. I hope you can see their log cabin someday. They bought the cabin at another site and moved it, log by log, to Wilsey Bay. They rechinked all the logs, bleaching the interior sides, and finished off the rooms with Darlene's flair for the eclectic. Since everyone was stopping at my less than chic cottage for the second half of the evening, I went all out with the decorations for the dessert table. "Southern Living" would have approved of the tasteful arrangement of fresh mums and other seasonals , , , after-dark cuttings from the neighbors' garden. Crime doesn't pay, however, because at the last minute I found I had not only stolen Absent Mary's leftover perennials, but also her last surviving insects. Hiding a saucer of vermouth amongst the larger gourds and realistic WalMart grapes took care of the bug stowaways as well as some fruit flies which were still flying around looking for the ripening banana I had replaced with the new clever decorations. Fortunately, such critters do not make sad drowning noises to alert the guests.

Dave and Jeff drove out to the camp on this beautiful Almost Fall day, and I know they are having a good time together in the woods and enjoying the leftovers from the dessert table. (the baked items, not the drowned ones) Next weekend I will go to Houghton to visit Tom, Pam and Kellee and, hopefully, see some of the Copper Country color. We will take one last pontoon boat ride, weather permitting, along the canal on Tom's "Floating Loan" before it is stored for the winter.

Hope you are home safe and sound again. Things may get a little dicey on the international scene in the next few weeks, I fear. anniecat, who is now domesticated, watches news broadcasts, but seems most animated when the Whiskas commercials are aired. Perhaps there is a wisdom in this sorting out what is really important. (*Barb tells me she and Earl both quit smoking during the Gulf War. Now she cannot hear CNN announcers without pain. Just the mention of scud missiles makes her start patting her clothing for a pack of smokes. This latest conflict must be hell for the Larsons as well as the Iraqis.*) Love from jojo and anniewisecat

02.10.5   Bernese Mountain Dogs

Beaufort Babs, Happy to hear the beach week was fun and educational; i.e. picking up hints on latest business attire. Where exactly do corporate men have their tattoos???? Be explicit . . . I am doing research.

I spent the weekend with Sandy O. and her three dogs. The one female was in heat and breeding at the motel between shows. Todd wanted to know which motel . . . he said he had this vision of big dogs bouncing on the beds, and didn't want to stay at that place. Met her and the four Bernese Mountain Dogs in Rapid River, and our caravan made its way to Soo, Ontario, Canada, adding Tammy and Madeleine Rose to our little troup. So, there we all were at an International Dog Show; only one of us knowing exactly what to do. But it turned out that three of us were merely the other end of the leash for a dog not waiting to be shown. This is not as insignificant as it sounds. We actually had to make sure the right dog got to the handler. When the judging picks up speed, and the male dog's lust has been denied too long and he shows unsportsmanlike behavior, there can be stress. Sandy seemed pleased with her (eventually) very hairy asst. handlers; and was delighted with the excitable male who won best of breed on his honeymoon. Tammy, Madeleine and I departed for the USA in triumph and a cloud of dog fur. Thank you for sharing Sandy O. with us. Love you, jojo

02.10.8   Rocky Mountain Hi

Burba,

So comforting to know I can reach you in the canyonlands. You said you left the RV behind to travel to Aspen ??? Do you rent cars??? Or are you backpacking across the Great Divide??? I enjoy this picture in my mind: You and Earl and other Sierra Club members pacing off the miles to the summit, carrying colorful backpacks, stopping occasionally to dine on greens growing from the rocks or to take big bites from your Chapstix. My carpenter has been and left, doing a beautiful job of sealing off my nest from the north wind. I am procrastinating as I write this . . . putting enamel on expensive new surfaces gives one nightmares of BRUSHMARKS! Perhaps an extra whiff of paint thinner before I begin will up my confidence level . . . or lower my expectations. Love from jojo

Oh dear, we got your suggestion for backpacking
the mountains too late. Before your letter
arrived, Earl disconnected the truck from the
RV and we drove the whole 560 miles. Drat!
We could have taken short cuts and made the

trip much shorter. Also a savings on gas
which was nearly $2.00 per gallon. Believe me
Chapstix would have been the only thing to
eat unless I might have stabbed a cow with my
paring knife. The drought is awful, mountains
beautiful. Aspen was wonderful. I had never
seen it without a full snow cover. We stayed
right downtown and walked to the Mother Lode
for a great meal and a bottle of Red Wine. I
said farewell to all the old ski hills as I do
not expect to make the hike again. Many good
memories. Love, Barbara

02.10.10   Into October

Barb and Earl, After a wild night of severe thunderstorms and tornado
warnings, we have a beautiful, clear October-like day to begin the
new season. The last dock on Squaw Point is gone, and we have geese
stopping daily to rest on the spit in front of my house . . . sleeping,
I suspect, with their beaks pointing South. It is a day to enjoy my
walk, knowing that my 3mpd will not be so pleasant soon . . . I will
go in to Gladstone this afternoon to be at the last cross country meet
this year for Abby and Molly. Both running well . . . Molly took 3rd
in the invitationals last weekend . . . her first year on the team. Abby
gamely competing as her jaw heals from further surgery to implement
her orthodontic work. Love to you both from jojo and annieautumncat

02.10.15

KODAK has done it to me again . . . . Flushed my self-esteem down
the toilet, destroyed my world of hot fudge and Hardee Curly Fries.
I've seen the photos of me taken in the Soo with our friends from
Florida. I am now a sworn member of Weight Watchers, Overeaters
Anonymous and Alcoholics Anonymous; taking diet pills, becoming
bulimic, and am on a waiting list at the Betty Ford for food addiction.

I have survived on two saltines since I saw the photographs. I plan to join the YMCA and Curves for Women as soon as they can get my stretcher through the door. Please write, but don't send food. Love, jo

```
Yes,  I   have  received  similar  photos  from
friends  .  .  .  especially  ones  taken  in  the
morning  as  they  depart  our  house.  They  in
fine  new  traveling  outfits,  me  in  a  ratty
bathrobe  and  tennis  shoes.  I  am  sitting  in
Pueblo,  Colorado,  where  it  is  so  dry  my  lips
are  cracking.  Tomorrow,  we  head  for  Aspen  but
leaving  the  RV  on  its  own  for  a  few  days.  Start
a  bonfire  with  the  pictures  and  cook  up  a  mess
of  s'mores.  Love,  Barbara
```

02.11.2   Anniecat and the Eagle

Water's edge in South Carolina must be lovely yet. The weather here has been remarkable . . . . could reach 60 again today. Fall has stripped the trees which makes the sunlight seem unseasonably strong. Sunday morning I awoke to a great commotion, and saw anniecat sitting out on one of the topmost branches of a tree near the beach. The neighbor's dog was pacing and barking below while calm kitty quietly gazed across the bay. I have watched versions of this game before. She will sit on a high perch, sometimes for hours, until the dog loses interest and wanders off. I imagine her little yawn just before she leaves her tree and disappears. That day, by the time I had poured my morning coffee, the dog had given up, but cautious cat remained safely (she thought) aloft. An eagle watched from the edge of a sandbar close to my shoreline. I dressed for church, but kept checking on the eagle which loomed, unmoving, in the binoculars, and on anniecat who appeared very fluffy and vulnerable in the bare treetop. Perhaps I really wasn't needed. As I've written, anniecat expects so little of me. However, I missed church because I spent the morning sitting under the tree, dressed in my best Lutheran suit, talking to the cat until she decided to come down and the eagle flew away. I was rewarded with one of anniecat's rare moments of spontaneous affection which left my Lutheran suit covered in cat hair and my heart filled with absolute gladness. jojo and anniehappycat

02.11.12   Caribou Meatloaf

Burba, It is 50 degrees!!!! A chance to give my windows another washing on the outside since that won't happen again for 5 more months. No wonder so many Yoopers have Seasonal Affective Disorder. Even when there is a good day in the middle of winter, their windows are so murky by then the world still appears to be grey and overcast. I have caribou meatloaf in the oven. How many of your friends can say that?? I spent yesterday afternoon at the library reading up on washing machines. I will go shopping with the money from sale of the dock. I certainly won't miss the dock as much as that one seagull and flock of ducks who used to roost on it as if they had rented it for the season. They now swim aimlessly in the empty shallows. Do you suppose I could have asked a better price if I sold it as a bird sanctuary? love from jojo and anniegettingfluffycat

02.12.16   Christmas Decorations

Burba and the Earl, While everyone is dreaming of a white Christmas, I can picture myself enjoying the turn of the tide from that little bench behind your house. My tree is settling under the overload of ornaments. I cannot leave one single piece in the boxes . . . from the most beaded and glittering to the limp little paper cutouts created by tiny hands so many years ago. Because each has its own story, I guess I imagine it also has its own soul and would be wounded if passed over. This was a good year for tree decorating. The string of lights which went out after the whole tree was decorated were at the bottom of the tree. All is decorated up to and including the door to the crawl space. I am Clark Griswold from 12/15 to 12/31. Have a joyful Christmas!!! Looking forward to seeing you in the New Year. Love from jojo and annieChristmascat

02.12.19   The Living Nativity

Burba: Tonight is our "Living Nativity" program at the church. Each year the children do a re-enactment of the Christmas story in front of the church with backdrop of plywood minor characters. These life size figures were found in my crawl space when I moved into this house. This is a story in itself. Anyway . . . they were brought to the church where each year during Advent they are placed among hay bales and mounds of snow, the area is surrounded by lights; and on one night the children become part of the scene, in the company of animals from local farms. Some years it has been very cold, but many of us remark on how wonderfully we see the stars on those frigid nights . . . and how beautifully the Word carries in the cold air.

I am finishing up the decorating now that I have been "laid off" from the meat plant. The tree is glorious, very fresh and fragrant . . . however, so large and heavy it fell over once totally lit. (we are still talking about the tree here) Carol's Kenny to the rescue and it was upright and secure again. This story I will not share with my friends who claim it's nonsense to keep cutting real trees.

I have all these little boxes of the pink Packer hats wrapped for my daughters-in law and granddaughters for Christmas. I had ordered them ages ago because they sell out as soon as a shipment comes in. Hoping they will still wear them with their Lions shirts. We had cousins here from SanDiego-Denver for their first Christmas with us in the Northwoods. A partial calendar of events reads: sleigh ride with big, gassy horses and the smallest cousins with only their eyes exposed to the weather, caroling at homes along the Stonington road while fortified with Swedish glog and Hawaina Johnson's butter spritz at stops along the way, Ryan's hockey games, Jeff and Laurie's famous open house (the world invited) featuring Amy, Abby and Molly's "cutout cookies" iced in experimental colors.

I don't remember if I took you down the road to see our little church in the woods. A Lutheran congregation plus one Presbyterian convert. Since it was built sometime during the era of birchbark canoes, it is high maintenance; and we are always one spaghetti supper or raffle away from bankruptcy. But, what happens every Christmas Eve only on Stonington makes Trinity Lutheran Church remarkable. For months, members of the congregation save empty gallon milk jugs in their garages. An old pickle jar is kept at the back of the church sanctuary to collect loose change which is then turned into special luminary candles. About the time the deer hunt begins to slow down, the jugs are each cut to accommodate a healthy layer of sand from our shoreline and a candle. During the afternoon of Christmas Eve, no matter the weather, the luminaries are placed along the road; and just before the church service that evening, the candles are lit. For nearly three miles, each side of County Road 513, from the township hall park to the steps of the church, we drive along a beautiful pathway of light to a service of carols. Many people drive over to Stonington just to experience the luminaries . . . and some find their way thus to our little church and its message. Merry Christmas.

02.12.27

Earl and Barb, I may or may not have sent you a card. Hopefully, I did. I mailed out all the Christmas cards this year, then discovered a card with a somewhat generic message written on it without an envelope. I'm assuming there was an empty envelope from me in someone's mailbox. I hear this sometimes works with the utility companies when you are stalling until your Social Security arrives. On the other hand, I received two cards with the same handwritten message from one of my friends this year. I also received one unsigned card, one card with postage due, and three that belonged to my neighbor which I kept because they had money in them. I also thought I let the cat out this morning, but discovered I hadn't. love from jojo and annieconfusedcat

03.2.15 Ft.   Lauderdale

Burba, Ft. Lauderdale. I have Scott's computer to work on. He thinks I make potato salad and wash windows for fun, so next week we are taking off for the Keys. Actually, it is so pleasant here at his place. I enjoy his little balcony over the river, and I have the peaceful Jackson for company during the day. I spent a week with MaryEllen in Stuart. She does love to entertain; and there was a karoke night, Super Bowl party and singing at the piano in the club. Good fun. I bought a peasant blouse and ballet slippers. Scott left his car for me today so I put on the sun oil, put the top down (on the convertible) and drove down to the beach, listening to steel drums on the radio and eating a luscious peach. I was so Florida. Will shop for flamingo margarita glasses and flipflops. Looking forward to seeing you again in a few weeks. I have shelved the stories for a while. If we paste them all together some day, you should do the serious stuff and I will put in the commas , , , Love from Consuela

03.4.10   Confused State

Barb: Not one single offer on my house, which makes me feel as if I have been living in a slum or worse for the past 14 years. I want to take naps which is not like me, leaving me to suspect I am depressed, that my furnace which runs constantly is emitting carbon monoxide or both.

Seeking DIVINE INTERVENTION (I think the Catholics may capitalize all this stuff), I have buried a statue of St. Joseph upside down in my front yard . . . a guarantee that the house will sell. This is not a tip passed on by any realtors, but whispered to me by a lady in Sayklly's where the statues are sold for $4.95 and $10.95. I have started out with the cheaper version, thinking perhaps DIVINE INTERVENTION is not based on race, creed or level of munificence. If St. Joe doesn't deliver, I am thinking I will keep the house listed until after hunting season, hoping some hunter may stagger out of the woods and sign a purchase agreement before he sobers up. My golf game has not happened yet . . . I have failed to cut the ties to U.P. real estate and I am not blond. I am so NOT Florida . . . perhaps this is a sign to me from poor St. Joseph who is somewhere upside down among the frosted hostas. Stay tuned.

03.4.20

Burba, I love the shirt with fun message thereon! You are the best . . . and I shall wear it, but not to the Swallow Inn as directed. Have to walk past the pool tables to get to the salad bar which means turning my back on the Rapid River contingent of NRA. Thank you also for the good airline reading. Will take my mind from the former terrorists lounging at the Detroit terminal newsstands.

While some still encourage me to put my house on the market and make a permanent move, I could not knowingly distress my children again . . . ever. I stop in to visit them and find silence (Jeff), supportive sadness (Laurie), tears and disappointment (the granddaughters and two Labradors). The other children have various painful emotions, too. I have unearthed St. Joseph, and relieved him of his vigil from beneath the hostas. I know it is I who will keep feet forever planted in Stonington—and am glad of it. jojo and anniegratefulcat

03.4.15   April

Dearest Burba, We haven't had a blizzard for 24 hours . . . Is this Spring? Since I have been home, we have had 3 days of sunshine (I counted). Saturday I drove to and from Marquette to call upon my soon-to-be-divorced-sister. Poor Sandy. I wanted to bring her home with me, but she will have to find her own way, just as we did. Worst driving I have ever done. Just me, two logging trucks and an ambulance on the road. Didn't even go to the Marquette Younkers Store Rock Bottom Get This Trash The Hell Outa Here Sale because I was snowblind and couldn't read the price tags (which is half the fun at a RBGTTTHOH Sale) So here I am waiting for this glacier I am living on to melt so that I can get to my garage without roping myself to various trees along the path from the house. But, if you will remember, April can be either the most hopeful or most disappointing month of the year in the U.P. Another week and I'll drag the dried out geraniums from the crawl space to get them started. This is the time of year when I have to keep myself from buying those little "water and grow" containers full of promising flowers seeds. I would have to put them somewhere in my limited space in this house which is still available . . . like on one end of the dining table (weekdays only) or the other half of my bed. love from jojo and anniecat

03.6.29 Breeze The Beast

You may remember my neighbors' Chesapeake, Breeze. Waaayyy over the weight limit at most hostels; therefore, she occasionally stays with me while her family travels. Breeze arrives with her own luggage filled with approved meals and treats, favorite toys and personalized dinnerware. She also comes with a supersize Cabela's dog bed which she doesn't sleep on. She sleeps on my bed. Arriving at my house, she walks straight to the bedroom to test the mattress as if checking into a Holiday Inn. We had the pleasure of each other's company for several days last week.

If I had Nancy's talent, I would have woven the leftover dog hair into a pashima or at least boxed it up to send to a charity for modest chihuahuas. Two hours before Breeze the Beast's owners were to reclaim her (fed, brushed, scented, with spot-cleaned collar), and just when I was feeling a little down while taking our last walk together, she had this idea about celebrating in a murky beaver pond. The celebration included at least one very surprised beaver and me (since I was attached to the other end of the leash). How does one top such fun? You must walk into the clean, COLD water of the bay to remove all traces of pond scum and beaver poop. The dog will enjoy this much more that you. Breeze went home a very happy dog, and I'm sure she is recommending me to all her friends who speak Chesapeake. Her family, pleased at seeing the dog so well and happy . . . or just grateful to have had a week without her . . . presented me with a very nice parting gift and flattering photo of Breeze "in case I miss her." I was thinking, initially, it was more like a useful reminder of how much I don't want another dog. But, I find I look at it more and more because I miss her. jojo

03.10.10   Anniversaries

Hi Beaufort Babe, Just a quick greeting. Am taking a break from the Great Pumpkin Project: that is, I am arranging pumpkins on the deck in a manner which (1) would fool my guests into assuming I have some decorative talent or at least the Halloween Spirit; and (2) is unappetizing to the local deer herds. Nancy and Bill celebrated their 48th!!!!!! wedding anniversary. Among all of the Soo Sisterhood, I am guessing they, with Fran and Elli Papineau, win the prize. They leave today for the Soo for their annual reenactment of their honeymoon on Sugar Island. Perhaps that is the secret. Dave's idea of a honeymoon would be to camp out in the back of his truck and fish a tournament for 14 hours a day . . . which is what we did, come to think of it. jojo and annieautumncat

04.1.3   Happy New Year

Burba, Leaving the Canadian border two days previous, and after dropping Scott off in Ft. Lauderdale, I arrived in Stuart, FL in time for a date with a Sailor on New Years' Eve. The shimmery glimmery dress had migrated to a corner of the trunk behind the beer cooler, but was restored, as was I, by a little steam from the shower. Then off to the ball. Sailor in a tux, champagne on the table, our fellow partygoers dancing and being festive. All men look handsome in a tux, and all women look good to men in tuxes when there is champagne on the tables. We even put on those silly hats. There was chocolate mousse with fresh raspberries for dessert . . . a perfect evening. I hope your New Year began as happily as mine. Best wishes dear friend. Jojo

04.4.4   A Few Miles On Her

Burba, Good weather prevailed, and I crossed the Smokies for the 8th time in one year, working on the same question I ask myself when I first see mountains ahead: Why didn't those pioneer women just unhitch the oxen and head back to the valley? Certainly, some must have, but the ones who endured those crossings are on my mind every time I sit in my air-conditioned/heated car, listening to Delbert cd's and scaling the summits on cruise control. Nine hours from Beaufort, and with a runny nose (a true indication I am headed north), I arrived in Richmond, Kentucky sometime after every cheerleader in the state. Trying to obtain a room during the state cheerleading competition by pleading I was, in fact, a participant did not work. Hard to pass as a cheerleader and still get your AARP discount. My friends from Richmond called to invite me to their home, but by then my virus and I were bedded down at a Brand X motel and trying to remember what promises I had made to the desk clerk in exchange for a room. Roland settled for treating me to breakfast next morning as I sneezed behind the Cracker Barrel linen.

I arrived in Stonington late that day, driving straight through, 13 hours from Richmond, where I left the dogwoods budding and pear trees blooming. Those marvelous horses, out to pasture now, stood in the lovely grasses of the Bluegrass State looking at me over miles of white fencing. I swear I tried to make eye contact with every one because I love each horse personally. Somewhere I heard they can sense that. Perhaps it was passed on to me by my borrowed horse Ginger, back in her stall at Meinrich Farms in Richmond.

The last two hours after the Bridge provided all the thrills of driving in the U.P.: wind-driven snow, 0 visibility, icy roads, deer, snowmobilers. I drank so much Mountain Dew to keep going that when I finally reached home and lay covered in bed with every quilt in the closet, wearing my entire Alaska Kayaking Wardrobe, my body twitched until exhaustion finally won out. I didn't keep track of the distance this trip, but when the sailors in the bars say I have a few miles on me, you may agree. Love, jojo

04.5.11   Stem Garden and Big Macs

Burba, I am raking and hauling debris, chopping out great clumps of winter-hardy marsh grass which has mysteriously appeared in my sad little garden of perennial stems. Perennial stems are common in this area of starving deer herds and devil bunnies who are always holding garden tours. U.P. Master Gardeners hold classes in identifying your plants without their foliage. This leads me to a new moneymaking idea:. Mystery tours of my garden's remaining stems. "Fun for the Whole Family . . . See who can identify the most dead vegetation! Score cards provided."

Here is a good story from local news last night. A large brush fire was threatening the edge of the national forest near Dollar Bay, and volunteer fire departments were called in to put down the blaze. The local McDonalds and Hardees donated food for the firefighters . . . which was brought to the remote area by easiest access. The Big Macs and Curly Fries were transported down a small waterway in kayaks. Only in the U.P.?? love, jojo and anniehelpercat

04.6.1   Getting Golf

Barb, I am, at last, finding people who will golf with me. Everyone says the same thing: I have no skills, just a lot of enthusiasm. I will play any cow pasture or back woodlot with anyone. I am not into placement or anything that resembles real golf. Hitting the ball then doing a little dance is still my thing. A group of ladies from Gladstone bravely include me in their weekly scramble. This is a good way for me to actually golf without incurring impatience or downright hostility from my teammates. They tell me if I can play Gladstone, I can play anywhere. Perhaps they forgot about me saying "Now What" so many times or whimpering about hitting a ball straight up a small cliff my kids used to ski off of for Gosh Sakes. I have been learning a lot from them, however, such as: how to cover the holes I have blasted in the sand traps; how to retrieve my ball from the creek, and how to clean the goose poop off the bottom of my golf shoes. I wonder if playing in Florida will be as much fun . . . where everything is so formal and groomed, and where I have to keep my shirt tucked in.

The remodel of the bath is (finally!) complete, and, since my tax refund paid for the project, I have dedicated it as the George W. Bush Room. Michael Moore did not attend the dedication. Love from jo

04.8.2   KOA's and PIRATE SHIPS

Jo, Last night, we were able to obtain reservations at the Petoskey KOA for Labor Day Weekend. What a surprise to find a vacancy! This means that when our boy sitting days at Kathy's in Alpena are over we can travel from Petoskey area to do some visiting, you included. What is the time factor from Petoskey to Rapid River? No plans as yet, just consider this a warning and don't change a thing that you have in the hopper. BofBB

Burba, YIPPEE!!! I am looking forward to having you and Earl here with me. Labor Day may be cool, and I will build you a little fire. It is a holiday, and so we will have to sit by it and enjoy refreshments (from glass bottles) to celebrate. Perhaps we will venture to the Swallow Inn to meet colorful citizens who will want to thank you for occasionally getting me out of town. I could plan a small dinner, including others,. Fishcalledwanda, my pet Beta, will entertain with amazing tricks learned watching Sea World commercials. You will not have throw pillows on your beds. Please, please come. I am 128 miles from St. Ignace. If you want, I will come and pick you up . . . . after you cross the high part of the bridge.

I am taking my photos of the past weekend in to WalMart to put them on a disc which perhaps I can forward to you by trial and error. I will provide commentary with same. For now, I will tell you they contain graphic material depicting families at this year's Bay Mills Rose Parade in pirate costumes piloting jetskis and all manner of floating transportation disguised as pirate ships, taken by me as I grasped the railing of the listing Rutledge "Black Pearl" after having downed the third glass of rum punch the crew and I drank from a bucket. More later . . . I drove home today with a headache from all the fruit in the punch. love jojo and fishcalledwanda

04.8.10 Shrimp Salad.com

Burba, Up at 3:45 a.m. to see Scott off . . . . waited around til 7:30 a.m. Plane broken. Flight cancelled. Back home to enjoy another day together . . . . probably napping. Try again tomorrow. Kim's departure on Sunday sorrowful but successful. Five days in a week at the airport and my face is now being depicted by sketch artists who try likenesses with dark beards. We had great fun the past few days. How I love my kids . . . !!!

Nancy and Bill arrive Friday after three days of Finn Food at the Marquette FinnFest. They may arrive late so am debating having "snack supper" or "casual chef's choice". Settled on a nice fresh-frozen shrimp salad. An alarming number of Yoopers are allergic to shellfish. I wonder if this could largely have to do with the preservatives used to ensure its safe trip all the way up here. Consequently, I'm cautious about menus for guests which include shrimp or crabmeat (lobster unheard of in our circles because we are leery of anything listed at "market price" . . . .) Anyway, will chance the shrimp, figuring Nan and Bill's immunity has to be impenetrable after all that Kuola-Maka and Lefsa. My recipes lack seafood salad ideas, evidenced my two days' search through mountains of all manner of pasta, gobs of mayo, two many capers, weird things like exotic sweet pickles or Thai spices which could be a secret antidote for allergic reactions. Most of these novel ideas for serving up a simple salad found on the internet. Got to be a game for me just running through the volumes of sites for recipes.shrimp salad. I will use my tried and true chicken salad mix, substituting shrimp from the depths of the freezer at Elmer's County Market, wishing I had not set my heart on this menu and had used the last day or so thinking about world hunger and cleaning up my house. Stay tuned. love, jojo and fishcalledwandasandy

04.8.20   Nancy

It was a Friday morning, and I scrubbed floors, polished the inside of the refrigerator, vacuumed under the beds (one should do that???). I pruned the shrubs, rearranged the woodpile, washed the outside of the garage. Nancy Kauppi Saunders was coming to visit. She of the grape vineyards, apple orchards, the house she remodeled herself and the antiques within (she has restored by learning carpentry and cabinetry). Someone once asked me after I had recited her accomplishments if she did her own dentistry. It is silly of me to try to impress Nancy. She totally knows me. We have been best friends since we first met in seventh grade. I look up to her like a sister; and we have always trusted each other with our happiest and sorriest secrets. Sixty years later, and all those miles between us, I am grounded by her voice. She is my link to the "Happy Days" between 12 and 21. Jr. Hi, Sault High, Western Michigan University, our little apartment on Pearl Street in Kalamazoo. She is like a destination in my world.

We had two delightful days. I gave her and the man we both love, "Wild Bill," the VIP tour of the Stonington Peninsula and Escanaba-Gladstone. Bill found a good book, a refrigerator with a few cold beers and was happy while Nan and I talked endlessly and drank up the wine. We cooked fresh walleye. Nancy presented me with an exquisite piece she had handstitched and appliqued on a boiled wool oval (she, of course, boiled the wool herself, but I'm not sure how one does this. I would certainly get out the soup pot, and next . . . .) It was then difficult to present my gift: a second edition of the "Stonington Recipe Box" cookbook, run off by Ginny Dahlin on the church copy machine and stapled together by Vacation Bible School children. I had, however, wrapped it in my very best piece of used birthday paper and crushed Christmas bow. I am still sleepless over this. She was very gracious, saying she thought most of the Swedish recipes in it were originally Finnish, and she would love trying some of them. It was hard to see them drive off, putting those miles between us . . .

All the family arrives on Saturday. Everyone will be dumbfounded by the freshly washed cans of Cream of Mushroom soup in the cupboard and the linen shelves I color coded last week !. jojo and fishcalledwandawhoisswimminginasparklingcleanbowl

04.12.6   Hunters/Fishermen/Hunters

Burba, You may have a hard time believing this, but a little over two weeks ago, some boats were still out in front fishing walleye. The deer hunters come here and do the early morning hunt, head onto the bay to fish until late afternoon and go back to the woods until sundown. The shore ice was well established before the last boat put out. Those hunters/fishermen certainly received their money's worth from their licenses this season! Then, it seemed as if within a couple days, the bay was frozen across, and my neighbors began hauling the fish shanties out onto the ice.

anniecat has moved to her retirement home in my nephew's house down the road from me. Having cared for her most of the past winter during my absence, Dan asked if she could remain with him as a housecat (a title she would highly dislike if she read email not addressed to her). This is a good arrangement all round. She now owns the entire premises, has two dogs to rule, goes to the groomer, and eats a prescription diet. Dan and I have reversed roles in that when he travels, I stop by his house to tend to the cat, during which times annie and I catch up on news and each other's health. But there are those evenings in my hair—and litter-free house, especially as winter comes on, when I sit with an empty lap and miss anniecat. Only jojo

04.12.15   The TREE

Burba, I worry about you Christmas shopping for Earl when you are not feeling well. I don't want you found sprawled behind a display of men's briefs. Better to faint away, if you must, in the HomeMedics section. I am decorating my TREE in sections. Jeff brought it in from the woods for me while I was away for the day. What a good kid. He must have moved all my furniture and my fine decorative pieces to get the TREE in a corner of the living room. It is a glorious tribute to Christmas. I'm thinking 10 feet tall . . . and about 6 feet wide. I right away had to get out the hedge trimmers and lop off a few branches so I could get to my refrigerator. It appears as if all the furniture is scrunched in one corner of the room as the tree looms omnipresent. And so, I hauled out the 12 foot ladder and tossed ornaments at the uppermost branches. When I light up that baby, the lights all over Stonington will dim; and our electric coop will have my photo on the cover of their next shareholders' report. Christmas morning we will all squeeze in around the TREE for a family gathering. God love you, Jeffrey Muggins. I picture him struggling with that TREE and the furniture and the knick knacks thereon, then restoring it all to order, vacuuming up the debris to provide me with this lovely, simply grand-smelling evergreen, dragged out of the snowy woods on a day when the wind chill on this peninsula neared 0 degrees. What a large and wonderful memory he has given me. Was it my imagination, or did it seem as if the TREE grew during the night???? Merry Christmas from jojo

05.2.1   Visiting the Sisterhood

Barb, Arrived home late afternoon yesterday. The neighborhood dogs had missed my handouts, and were at the back door barking happily. Was a very festive evening after a long journey which had begun in Ft. Lauderdale. The good wishes for a safe trip must have been sincere because I missed the big pileup in Grand Rapids by 9 minutes. Over 80 cars caught in a whiteout entering 131 where I had passed shortly before. I know the snow came onto me suddenly, and there was 0 visibility. Fortunately, I drove out of the squall after a brief time. Evidently, those behind me were not as fortunate. I drove in and out of gusting snow until Manistique, and arrived home tired but happy to see the sun shining over Stonington. Rita and I had a good visit. Talked endlessly and drank her special Turkish coffee . . . Reverse those words: we drank Turkish coffee: thus, talked endlessly. She would like to plan a trip to Albania late summer with a cousin who will help her with the travel. We stayed away from political subjects (she's still a Libertarian), and did not mention any men who have disappointed me (she claims to know Albanian assassins). Her eye problem is really life-altering, but we filled in the gaps with lots of happy memories and that good coffee . . . Drove over to Grand Rapids to have lunch with Grace who is recovering from a chipped kneecap after a fall on the ice. She is not very talkative about her health, so now you know as much as I do. Otherwise, she looks very Grace. Quietly stylish and such good company. Then on to Nan's in Kalamazoo. Her house is beautifully interesting and full of good antiques and Nan's flair for decorating with her own sewing, quilting, woodworking. She dresses beautifully . . . . most of her clothes made by her hand from Salvation Army castoff materials which she has "felted" "appliqued" or Heaven knows what to create a jacket, shirt, little shrug, etc. Even sitting in the evening, she knits or binds together knitting she has already completed. I tried to look busy marking pages in the TV Guide or brushing Kleenex lint from my old black slacks. The nice thing about longtime friends is you can pick up a conversation after months of separation as if you have merely stepped away for a few minutes. You and I have the opportunity to do that, and I look forward to being with you again soon. Bill played banjo and mandolin and we sang and laughed and told stories. Oh, yes, and Nan took me on a tour of Western Michigan U. Was like: "There is hardly a landmark I recall." Building after building . . . all new. When Nan and I were students the enrollment was 5,000. This year it is 30,000+. A great trip. Love, jojo

05.3.10   Sandy Sees Savannah and Fish Whisperer

BBofB . . . How gracious you are . . . If you knew how much I will truly enjoy seeing you, and just sitting under one of your lovely oak trees out back!!! Thank you for your welcome, and for sharing BB with me once more. And thank you to little sister Sandy for making this a fun trip . . . she is so excited that she is already counting the "sleeps" until we are underway. We won't drive into Florida. We are both looking forward to the visit with you, and will spend an extra day South in Savannah . . . or as you suggested, Charleston. Then we'll just take our time driving back. fishcalledwandasandy already has her reservation at Auntie Carol's. She considers this something like a trip to Sandals, since her bowl sits on Carol and Kenny's bar, and you know how she loves happy hour. This is a very wet and cold spring. Flooding again in Keweenaw, and the Rapid River threatens to cut me off from civilization to the south. Great amounts of water have pooled in the designated wetlands, and I have as many ducks swimming around in the back woods as on the bay out front. Soon! Jojo and FCWS

Jo, I am having problems with a Siamese Fighting Fish being called WandaSandy. I think he loved being at Carol's bar because they probably called him stuff like 'Butch' and 'Big Guy'. Probably gave him a shot with his beer. I am now lustfully reading the "Dog Whisperer" which followed the Horse Whisperer. When they come out with the Fish Whisperer, I will send it at once. I think only gold fish are called Wandasandy. Burba

BBofB,

I have real news for a change. MaryEllen called last evening . . . Just when I started looking for her picture on those party-size wine cartons . . . . As we guessed, she has been busy with Miles Grant business, but mostly wanted to let me know about three new men who had moved into the community. I now have their complete physical and sartorial descriptions, and a verbatim duplication of all conversations with these happy windfalls. If only I had 1/3 of her energy!!! Unfortunately, she called 4 minutes before the "Sopranos" premiere, so I had to ask her if I could cut out for a while, which was good because she had an opportunity to catch her breath and gather new chunks of conversations from memory . . . . during which Tony Soprano was shot, my three granddaughters came in on various airlines for spring break and the straw poll announced Frist was running first . . . and then I returned the call to pick up where we left off at the Miles Grant clubhouse.

Our weather has turned wicked. It is nearly 10 a.m. and dark as dusk . . . sleeting, freezing and very windy. We should have 8 inches. Hoping this is our "big storm" for March which usually comes in around St. Patrick's Day . . . . and that next week the weather will turn favorable so that Sandy and I can drive South without following a snowplow. Meanwhile, she has begun the countdown with me, and I am beginning to peek into my "summer dresser" where the sad leavings I call my warm weather wardrobe are stored. Happily thinking of you, Earl and Jackson. love, jojo and fishcalledwandasandy (who, by the way, thought your notes re a Fish Whisperer were so clever)

05.4.20   The Green Zones

Burba, Two loooooonnnnnngggggg weeks have passed since my foot surgery. With the initial suffering over, I go mad to put my foot down. I must carry the mending foot away from earth and hop along on crutches, putting all weight on my fake hip. It is cozy in my recliner where I look at photos in "Golf" magazines and read endlessly, venturing occasionally into the "green zones" in the house which I have cleared for my crutches by falling into obstacles heretofore situated therein, fragments of said objects now scattered across the landfill. I see the dr. this week, and, hopefully, he will begin to wean me from the crutches and let me at least put a heel to ground again. This would make it much easier to get my brookies (a reference from my latest reading on civil war in Rhodesia) up and down in the bathroom without ripping off the shower curtain as I fall into the shower stall (which is out of the green zone). Your, jojo

05.5.10   Pencil in Abby

Burba, I began keeping a calendar recently. I have so many events scheduled, I write things down. This is pretty exciting, considering notable commitments to date included my dental checkup and rotating the tires. Rita will be with me from June 1 to 5. There is no sign of "carpenters" on the little squares before those dates, so we will sit on my falling down deck and dodge the shingles popping from my falling off roof. I suppose the work crew will arrive on one of the days where I have visitors written down, together with a penciled in menu. Abby's graduation/birthday will be held tomorrow night, preceded by a family dinner (note "festive family menu"). Fortunately, in time to accommodate my calendar, the appliance store has received the replacement knobs for the stove burners which fell off while I was waiting to replace the stove. Neighbor boy Kyle's graduation party is next weekend (write down "double batch of baked beans"); and a cocktail party in Gladstone with my sailing friends I know Rita will want to meet ("gourmet appetizer"). This gets me through the next week and a half. Then I will begin planning for the family pre—and post—events when Kim, Scott, Tom and family arrive for the graduation party Jeff, Laurie and Molly are planning for Abby's graduation ("entire cookbook and two aisles of the Super Value"). Meanwhile, I have postponed the dental checkup to a time when I have nothing else to write on the little date squares, and I missed the appointment at the tire shop because I was penciling in my calendar. jojo

05.6.1   Memorial Day

BBofB, We are nine hours into Memorial Day. It is not raining at this time, and in one hour the ceremony at our little church cemetery will begin. This year those old soldiers who come from the Rapid River VFW and American Legion can stand in the sunshine they deserve. The parade in downtown Rapid begins at 1:00 p.m. Our Stonington Booster Club's entry in the Memorial Day Queen contest has tough competition this year from the Alger Delta Electric Coop contestant. I am making my scroodle noodles to pass at our family picnic hosted by Ken and Carol. As a special surprise, I will try to make the Joe Frogger cookies they all like. The recipe calls for 1/2 cup of rum, and I try not to start the cookies too early in the day because I may have a convenient cup of coffee sitting around yet when I get to the rum part.

My carpenters finally were honest with me and declared they would not be able to do my projects THIS YEAR. Well, &*%##%*!! But, I played the sweet little old lady and said that I understood, and would they please put me first on the list for next year, give me an appointment card signed in a first grandchild's blood, and I would have the contract I will put out on them next spring cancelled as soon as I hear hammering on my roof. It's enough to drive one to Joe Froggers. love from jojo

05.6.2   Edging the Sidewalks

Burba, I am edging my sidewalks with an old butcher knife. Everyone who stops by to find me kneeling in the dirt, surrounded by armies of ants declaring war, slicing away at years of sod, tells me there is a tool for this. I know this. But the challenges are: I either buy a tool of occasional need, drive to town and rent one, find a lender somewhere in Stonington who has sidewalks and is generous. I just kneel down and cut the sod away, and for a couple of days ignore everyone telling me there is a tool for this. The finished edging looks like I don't take advice. The ant bites on my legs are painful, but it's my project and I say it's going well. Next, I have to take out a dead oak tree with my three-corner saw . . . something I learned from Rita Prohazka. (Barb's mother)

In the evenings, I attend meetings at the church as we seek to find a new pastor. At our last meeting, the Bishop came from the U.P. Vatican in Marquette to pray with us Leaderless Lutherans . . . the lost sheep of the Synod . . . but alas, had no available ministers or future graduating seminarians who want to relocate to halfway down CR 513. We pray for an indigent retired minister or an LLM (licensed lay minister). I'm thinking I should encourage my grandchildren to give up chemical engineering and finance to become ministers. Apparently a wide-open field with great perks, and "did God's work" is the kind of thing you want to have them read off your resume when you knock on the Pearly Gates.

6/18 Sunday I drove into town to see Jeff, Laurie and girls join the Presbyterian Church, thinking: well . . . I'll hear a good old Presbyterian sermon again. There was a visiting minister that Sunday, however. You guessed it: a pastor from Bethany Lutheran. But the coffee in the Social Hall tasted Presbyterian. I hope they aren't making it in aluminum pots. I haven't heard from MaryEllen. She called from atop the Mackinac Bridge, probably at that part where I drive with my eyes closed. She claimed she was going straight to Bay Mills. Perhaps she has run off with a classmate there, and is at this very moment watching a NASCAR race. I will call you when I find my phone. I think the ants carried it off so I couldn't call for help. love jojo

05.6.15   Auntie Carol

Wouldn't everyone enjoy waking each morning to that beautiful smell of baking? Carol Beggs Mosher and her two brothers grew up one flight of stairs from the family business in Escanaba—Thompson's Bakery. She recalls the fragrance of her father's famous "bear claws" and coffee cakes, rising breads, large copper pots of custard and melting chocolate. On school mornings, Carol's mother, readying the shop below for customers, would stop to bang on a pipe to waken the children. Stanley and Hazel Beggs began their day at 3:00 a.m. Though their children were able to help with the operation of the bakery, and their summer jobs were just downstairs, each decided on a different livelihood. Carol chose teaching, receiving her degree from Western Michigan University in 1957.

Teaching first in Birmingham, Michigan and then Racine, Wisconsin, Carol moved to Green Bay where she taught kindergarten/first grade for twelve years, during which time she had a warm friendship with her neighbors, former Packer defensive lineman Henry Jordan and his wife, Olive. The Jordans often included her in gatherings with other Packers, and Carol tells of once walking out their shared entrance to find a conversational Paul Hornung sitting on her steps. She helped out with the Jordan children, and is kidded by her family who refer to this time as her Packer babysitting days . . . complete with fringe benefits for everyone back in Escanaba, such as great seats for games and autographed footballs Henry had passed around at practice during those glory days of the late sixties.

Carol's family tree became firmly planted on Stonington when her great-grandfather, Charles Beggs, was commissioned the first lighthouse keeper at Peninsula Point shortly after the end of the Civil War, during which he had served as a sailor. Her grandfather was born in the lighthouse. And so, in 1970, Carol accepted a teaching position in Ford River allowing her to return to the Upper Peninsula and take up residence in the family cottage on Stonington, where she and her husband Ken Mosher II . . . 31 years, three children, six grandchildren, two dogs, three cats, and countless remodelings and renovations later . . . still reside.

When she and Ken were married in 1978, he brought three children to the marriage, Kenneth III, Jeff, and a daughter, Kerry. The two boys came to live with them shortly after their marriage. Years later, after the death of their birth mother, Ken's sons wanted to recognize Carol's role in raising them, and sought to "adopt" her legally. There being no real legal example for this, the court recommended a hearing, and one morning the Mosher family drove to the courthouse where the boys were officially granted their wish to acknowledge Carol's devotion to their care and upbringing. Now, with families of their own, Ken III and his wife, Cari, have three daughters, Megan, Emily and Hannah; Jeff and his wife, Melissa, have a son, Perrin, and daughter, Cienna. Kerry has two children, Ashley and Robert.

An avid seamstress and crafter, Carol is a natural for quilting. She began experimenting with designs and colors and was soon creating quilts for family and friends. Shortly before her retirement from teaching, Carol and Ken were in town shopping for groceries and bought a log cabin, which followed them home to Stonington. Carol's little cabin on County Road 513 has become a local landmark as the home of School Bell Crafts, a market for her beautiful quilts as well as local art, basketry, woodwork and craft items produced by her neighbors. No commissions or consignment fees change hands, and Carol pays all taxes. Her goal, originally, was to justify to Ken all those bolts of material sitting around the house, but, ultimately, grew into a testament to her business abilities and the energy she puts into promoting community life in Stonington. This energy radiates to the Stonington Booster Club, the Bay de Noc Township Review Board and elections committee, and spreads into helping promote activities at the new township hall . . . . from decorations to polka party food and conversation during the hall's morning "coffee club."

Aside from her family, Trinity Lutheran Church receives the greatest share of Carol's enthusiasm and good works, including serving on the Altar Guild, as an usher and offering counter and choir member. She puts aside a week each June to help with Bible School, importing her own granddaughters from Minneapolis to participate. She can make volcano cupcakes when called upon. She has been President of Ladies Aid for over 20 years. If that, in itself, isn't some sort of record, consider the number of hot dishes, salads and cakes she has amassed, phone call by phone call, to provide funeral meals for Trinity Lutheran's families. She doesn't keep count, but does recall more than once she and her group of volunteers transported all the dishes, flatware, tablecloths and the food to churches in Escanaba and Gladstone by request. It is a somber responsibility being one of the first to hear of a death in our congregation, but Carol will tell you providing the comfort of food and fellowship for a grieving family is truly a labor of love.

Which brings us back to quilts. Carol wasn't among the first group of Monday morning quilters, but in recent years, she has taken on most of the responsibility for their survival and success. The cutters, piecers, sewers can count on her being there before 9:00 a.m. Monday mornings with all in readiness for a morning of work and friendship. On a Sunday each May, Trinity Lutheran celebrates its annual "Blessing of the Quilts" and pie social, instituted by its quilters to share their work with the congregation and, through their pie sale, to raise money for materials. This year, 58 quilts will be brought to Bay Cliff Health Camp. Previously, quilts have been placed on beds at the VA Hospital in Iron Mountain and the Jacobetti Center for Veterans in Marquette. Members of the Trinity Lutheran congregation who are facing serious illness or crisis receive a quilt with the words chosen by the quilters to accompany their gift . . . *"May its warmth comfort you, and its colors cheer you. This quilt was sewn for you with joy and*

love by the Trinity Lutheran Church quilters in Stonington, Michigan."
Spread out over the Upper Peninsula from young campers' cots to old
soldiers' hospital beds, a colorful legacy of service carried out "with
joy and love" includes Carol Mosher's touch.

05.7.2   Save the Spode

BBofB, The Mega Millions drawing is up to $170 million today. I lay
awake last night thinking of how I would distribute such wealth. You
and Earl, of course, made the list. Happy dreams just piled up, not the
least of which was the realization I could buy a place down the street
from you and we would drive our Porsches to the book store and buy
HARD cover NEW releases. We could have marvelous dinner parties,
catered, and we would rent such guests as George Will to listen to and
Johnny Depp to look at. I woke up this morning vowing to buy a ticket
when I go to town to drop off my garbage in Jeff's cans and leave off
my overdue library books.

Temps in the 90's and no rain in weeks. My worries about my dry
lawn and trees have grown to real concern for the entire peninsula
which is crackling dry. One little spark out there and I throw the Spode
and my kids' baby photos in the paddleboat and start pedaling from
shore. This plan passed on by my sons, minus the time for the dishes
and photos.

Hoping you have a great time on Daufuskie Island. Will you visit
Conroy haunts? I have the bridal shower thing coming up, but Friday
nite the FAARPS and I are going to the Gladstone Golf Club for a fish
fry and cold beer on the deck overlooking the Days River . . . where
most of my golf balls have found a new home. I actually won a little
ball with a painted on life jacket for making the biggest donation to
the river, an indication of the progress I have made learning the
game. But I have made lots of new friends, probably because I make
everyone who plays with me feel like a really great golfer. love, jojo
and fishcalledwandasandy (who has a middle name now because I
learned Sister Sandy had named her dog after me and I felt I should do
something nice for her)

05.7.20   Petunias and Pasta Pots

I am so happy to have a free day to write letters and play Free Cell on the computer and clean our shower with the new shower thing-e-do called Bath Wand which I highly recommend to all my pals. On the schedule is a trip to Daufuskie Island to celebrate your Birthday.

Last Friday, we went off our medication and ordered up

tickets, motel and airplanes for the Packers game in Green Bay on 9/25. Our life savings going blithely off to Lambeau for two seats on about the 25 yard line. Love B of BB

05.8.2

Have fun at Daufuski with your friends on my birthday. I'm spending the beginning of my next year at a bridal shower, struggling to do those wedding anagrams with my aging brainpower and being polite about avoiding the fruit punch. I prefer being invited to the bachelorette parties where they serve real drinks and enjoy male entertainers who . . . . well, let's say I wouldn't need brainpower. Now that kind of social planning would get them a big shower gift from me.

I'm cautiously happy about your tv advertised BathWand after my experience with the PastaPot. The night I had ALL my children and grandchildren for dinner a few weeks ago, (the night I served the deformed meatballs I had to cut the overdone bottoms off of) I presented the draining of the pasta like some GD Vegas spectacular as everyone finished their salads, saying: "Watch this handy pot I bought for $19.95, plus shipping and handling," turning the pot over as the top came off and every last noodle went into the sink. Remember to read instructions on wonder gadgets and practice when no one is looking and always have a clean sink. (this you may be able to ensure with a BathWand!) Greatly unlike you, my entertaining has hit new lows. Dessert for everyone the other night was a Klondike bar, still wrapped in frosty foil, dealt around the table to each diner by your gracious pasta princess like the first card in a losing hand. Love from jojo and fishcalledwandasandy

05.8.2   Firewalls

Burba, My Nephew, Deej, returned the pc last night in exchange for 4 dozen of my peanut butter cookies, a tuna casserole (his favorite), and red jello with cherries in it. A real barter for me because he has installed firewalls, downloader detectors, anti-virus programs, etc. etc. etc. I feel safe in saying that you may now reach Sec'y Rumsey's inbox with less difficulty than breaking through to anniecat. (be sure to attach proof of your identification with a recent photo to all letters mailed to my email address; and if you wish to forward any jokes, cute puppy pictures, or inspirational stories. these must be cleared by the FBI, CIA, NATO, and the AAUW; all redneck humor must also be filtered by the Stonington Booster Club).

Will let you know about my new life at the Gladstone Golf Club where I will be spending two mornings a week, doing what I do best . . . not being the best, but doing my best. They have icy cold LaBatts at the bar; and tho I have never been much of a sudser, I find that beer can drown out a lot of disappointing putts, and washes down a lot of black flies that get caught in your throat. That's the story I'll tell the arresting officer. Have a good week. love from jojo

```
05.8.2
```

```
I want you to know that before I could read
your letter my computer had to check it out
with the DNR. No bugs were found or illegal
fishing licenses so the letter was allowed
```

to pass to my firewall. Since there was no description of hot sex in the Rapid River area, no alerts occurred and your message was then sent to be decoded. It was quietly passed on by AARP which means that you and I have a really dull life. Yes, I spent last weekend dealing with a new set of security codes to which I have now forgotten all the passwords. This may be your last letter from me before I explode. It used to be so easy! Earl thinks he is doing swell but we have no proof of that. We leave in the rv to explore a new vista. Friends say it is indeed, mosquito swamp. The nice Park near Key West is $100 per day.

That is steep when you are furnishing your own bed and bath. Anyway, I always enjoy getting away from the firewall for a few days. If you do not hear from me for a spell it is not because I am stuck in your anti-virus goo. Your letters will now be about your balls, and drivers, and back nines, and improving your swing, and lunch at the 'CLUB. However, your old friends will remember you fondly when you once wrote poems, novelettes. Love, B of BB

05.8.3   Bluefish Key

Dear Barb, I should have given up on poetry years ago. I am too "untaught" . . . But every once in a while the muse whispers . . . The following was composed between the produce section and bakery shelves at Elmer's Mkt. There was this cart and it had a defective wheel, so that the following came to me not in good form, but with rhythm: I wish that you had known me (clunk clunk clunk) when I lived on Bluefish Key (clunk clunk clunk) etc. jojo

I wish that you had known me
       when I lived on Bluefish Key.
My hair grew long and shiny
       and I slept beside the sea.
I read good books, drank pleasant wine
       and dined on fruit and greens.
I bathed in frangipani scent
       and dressed in faded jeans.
Each day I ran the simmering strand
       to meet the surf's embrace,
and like two lovers intertwined,
       we moved in rythmic grace.
The chitter of the dolphins' song
       rose through the dappled light
While tinkling crystal wind chimes
       conversed each zephrus night.
The kiss of brine upon my lips
       and warmed by tropic sun,
Inhaling breaths of water wind,
       my soul and sea were one.
That was my time of easy love,
       of living wildly free.
I wish that you had known me
       when I lived on Bluefish Key.

05.9.1   Three Barbies

Burba, Remember the summer of three Barbies? Barb Sterling and two of her friends, also named Barb, vacationed at the Bay Mills Casino. They may still be fondly recalled by regulars at the nightspots on the reservation. I heard Barbie II died suddenly two weeks ago. Always I wished I could be a little like her. At the age of 7?, she wore her shirts tucked into her jeans. She always dressed with a little glitter . . . some sequins on her blouses or beaded t-shirts, and expensive chandelier earrings. She owned a pair of real cowboy boots. I was looking forward to Barbie II driving up from her home in St. Petersburg, FL to stay at the casino for a week before our class reunion, during which we would hit golf balls off the Wild Bluff toward Lake Superior, hang out at the casino bar and generally eat, drink and be merry while I admired her boots. She woke up one morning, put on her makeup, and just dropped out of this world. We all knew she had a big heart, but none of us, including Barbie, knew it was on a timer. I am wearing earrings lately with my painting "shirt of many colors" as a small tribute . . . . love from, jo and fishcalledwandasandy

05.9.10   Missions

Jojo, I am so sorry that I have been such a poor correspondent lately. We have taken on the mission of trying to get help to a Baptist Church in Bay St. Louis, Mississippi. That is the beginning of the story and the end is that we will have to drive there. Would probably go this weekend if we were not going to Green Bay to view Lambeau Field and sell our Packers stock and set up a stand to dispense used packer wear. Does this hint at disenchantment or at least temporary disappointment?

The mission work has led me to sights that I cannot believe. The town is sticks and stones.

They will not even have a post office anymore because there is no place for mail to go and no one to send it. A Catholic priest was in Ireland during the storm and when he came back he had no home, no church, no car, no congregation. Now I have gotten as far as the Mayor's phone number (Ed Farve, naturally) and that phone rings so maybe I will get news from him some day. I am having a hard time having fun and thinking about what I have seen and read.

I suppose there will be no cancellations at the Settle Inn in Green Bay. It looks good, and even has a bar and grill and pool where I suppose we will all drown our sorrows after the game. Love, BofBB

05.9.12

Barb, Just made another call to the Settle Inn. I think they are beginning to recognize my voice, so am trying to discern if it is pity or hostility I hear coming at me. I've tried sorta disguising myself: refined lady (they didn't buy it); young and sweet (there was suppressed laughter); sultry (hearty laughter); sad and pleading (they cut me off). I will try my **loud Swallow Inn Whiskey voice** next. This may cost me my phone service, but am willing to give them one more chance.

Weather is warm and somewhat muggy . . . just so unusual for Stonington. There is a downpour of acorns and dead leaves, and every mouse and squirrel who knows what's coming is packing up to winter at my house. I have surrounded myself with mousetraps, resulting in a sad abundance of dead mice to discreetly dispose of in the empty lot next door. Thus, the appearance of unfamiliar stray cats skulking about, trying to find a way into the mice mother lode. I miss anniecat. Today I miss you more. I heard this morning from my friend in Houston that he has undergone the surgery to remove a malignant tumor, and begins treatment next week. Such a lovely, big and golden man, with this big booming laugh he used often; who would pick you up and swing you around just because he was glad to see you. I am out of words right now and sad. jojo

05.9.18   Fish Bowls and Favre

Big family dinner at Jeff and Laurie's tomorrow night. Abby's first visit home since August. She is doing well at Michigan Tech and says she likes it . . . . we all like that she pulled a 99% on her first math test. My fall bout with allergies has died off to small coughing fits and nasal speech, and I believe I am practically cured . . . . thanks to something I call "Pasta Remedia" and Rice Krispie bars. Now, if I can just get my jeans zipped up, I'm off to take some more boards from the old deck while the Rice Krispie Bar Rush is still on. love from jojo and fishcalledwandasandy (who is swimming happily in my big crystal salad bowl because I broke her jar last time I was cleaning it and haven't been shopping since. Try not to think about this next time you are here for salad.) Do you have news of Lambeau Field and Favre?

Oh, JoJo, how can it be so wonderful to have a friend who is right on top of the latest in epicurean delights. I understand that a number of famous chefs in New Orleans also have fish in their salad bowls. The French Quarter is rife with this wonderful treat. There you are in Rapid River right on top of the whole thing. Gourmet magazine will soon get a copy of my letter regarding your fast response to the trend.

Brett is really neat looking. Wonderful buns. He stood alone, with his back to our seats during most of the game. No one came and talked to him. As you know, the defense was on the

field most of the game. So Brett was just there
by himself. It was sad. BofBB

05.9.20   Molly's Last First Things

BBofB: How are you faring with Ophelia so close? I watch the
weather channel, and it appears as if part of that spinning blotch
which causes the forecaster to lower her voice is on your area of South
Carolina. Our hot, muggy weather was blown to the east last night
during a ripsnorting (do people say that outside Rudyard city limits??)
thunder, lightning, wind storm. Made the mice in the woodwork very
agitated and scratchy, and we all spent a restless night. Today is very
cool, and I am weeding out the front closet, hoping to find a somewhat
fashionable coat I forgot about. No luck, but I did box up all the
unfashionable coats I remembered, and brought them to my neighbor
for her yard sale. The cross country ski boots will soon be a memory,
together with the little box of ski waxes I liked the smell of. And I
hope someone appreciates the yellow fannypack which went to Alaska
with me. The cooler weather is energizing.

The coming weekend is homecoming, and I will spend two whole
days watching Molly on the drumline and/or twirling the flags in the
Flag Corps during the parade and game and before gliding down the
stairs in her homecoming finery. These senior days, she speaks of all
things as her LAST, such as: her LAST first game (think about that for
a second or two), her LAST cross country meet, etc., etc. So the family
must attend all these LAST events en masse out of love for Molly and
to grab up memories of her like precious treasure abandoned in her
wake.jojo and fishcalledwandasandy

05.12.7   Molly Running

She is a sturdy toddler in wee pink tights.

Laughing through little pumpkin teeth,
ribboned pony tails each side of her face bouncing,
Molly waddly-jogs down the hall toward me,
energy and joy with outstretched baby arms.
Running.

Launching herself from first base,
signals and calls fade around her.
At ten, Molly is a budding runner,
working on her "Phoebe" sprint.
Arms and legs in synchronized chaos,
she manages second, thrashes past third
and begins her slide to home.
Gritty clouds drift over the bay.
The crowd begins to cheer.
Who can refuse a dusty little legend?
She earned her piano
Running.

In a stinging October rain
I see her leave the woods behind
and start across the sodden field.
Body straining toward the finish,
Molly races over rocks and rain-slick leaves
on the far reaches of the Keweenaw.
She is determined to do her best,
knowing she is not the fastest.
It isn't the sunny, clear trail
we had hoped for her this day,
but, with purpose and resolve,

Molly meets the challenge.
Running.

She will know about rough, rocky, paths
and weariness and not being first.
But, Molly will always see the finish line
or just the end of the hallway as a goal.
She knows it's not how beautifully
or how fast you run . . .
It is about the desire to run
toward something with your whole heart.
And she will always have love within her arms' reach.

Radiant and timeless in ivory on prom night,
she wears pink grown-up gloves and the classic smile.
"Hi. I'm Molly. I'm nice," she would say.
So many images stored in our hearts . . .
from the dimpled knees in wee tights,
the long, mud spattered legs,
to these tanned limbs set in sequined shoes.

A gramma's practiced eye can spot
the smallest scrape on the knee
and the most painful bruise to her heart.
So, as she turned to leave, I saw them . . .
the smallest bits of my Molly memories
on the back of each heel.
With all the silk and netting,
beauty and poise,

the tiny marks from her running shoes.

Happy 18th Moll Doll.

06.4.4   Inbox and Author Friend

BB of B: Returned from the trip South to find 58 email messages, including: a delightful letter from you, 56 bulletins re male enhancement, outlawed video games, and the electronic notice to pay my internet fee, ensuring receipt of the aforesaid bulletins for another month. Did I acquire these unwanted solicitations when I signed up for AARP???

I am glad we both read Bill McPherson's books. I like to tell my family that my co-editor on a school paper went on to earn a Pulitzer. Whether this confirms that I am a pitiful underachiever or elevates my standing by association has not been mentioned.

I leave for Houghton Friday with granddaughter Amy Jo for Tommy's BIG 50 birthday party. Could I tell everyone he is my eldest and I acquired him on ebay when I was 10 years old?? The good news is that he and Pam are at the bank today to arrange to buy a very nice piece of property just down the road from me. A waterfront cottage with 5+ acres to the back of property and a pole building to store their boat. I hope this works out for them because this will be their summer place and, later, their retirement home. This brings love from jojo and fishcalledwandasandy/spike (who has learned he is a male)

06.4.20   Squaw Point Awakening

BBofB, My first nice long walk down the road this morning. It is sunny with temperature in the 50's. There are birds and smaller critters in the brush, a fishing boat on the bay. This is just the best—before wood ticks and mosquitos and, hopefully, bears. Was slow progress to my turnaround at Squaw Point. Many of my neighbors have returned from their winter retreats, and I found them at the road replacing the mailboxes carried off by snowplows, carting fallen branches from their decks and walkways or shoveling down the last stubborn snowbanks onto the lawns to melt. Service trucks come and go. Plumbing is reconnected, phone service restored, landscaping is underway. Carrying an armful of perfect pussywillows, I returned home to begin raking (what I think to be the leaf graveyard of Delta County), looking for new hope in my stem garden.

By now it is Tuesday, and a "town" day. I have my little list of groceries and reminders of overdue books. Today, however, I will have new adventures in the building supply boutiques. I am narrowing in on a carpenter, and he has asked me to "shop" for the shingles and windows he may actually come to install. I understand I am not qualified to touch these items, merely select and put them on another list.

The BIG 50 party for Tommy was a wonderful success . . . ended at 4 a.m., and I am thinking a few may still be sleeping off the celebration. There was talk of a mass grave and memorial services when I left Sunday morning. Pam must have cooked for weeks. Only 10 jello shots were left over from the 350 she prepared. Those were probably my allotment. As mother of the birthday honoree, I limited my overindulgences to everything on the menu. Hope you are having a good week. I am reading "Mermaid Chair" and looking forward to what develops with the monk. love from jojo and fishcalledwandasandyspike

06.6.8   Capt's Cabin

Burba, The Big Ass Ham cookout is now history. I fed the ham to 15 enthusiastic diners and had much left over, which gives you an idea of how big a big ass ham is. Tom and Pam have set up their cabin on Stonington! We all took turns hauling furnishings. It is so cozy and just really . . . . cabiny. Huge lilac trees blooming all around it right now delighted Pam. With all the windows open in this lovely weather, the whole cabin was fragrant with their scent. Jeff and Laurie stayed overnight at my place, and was just a great family time. These are the moments when you stop for a moment and say, "Thank you, Lord, for this happiness." There is much history attached to the property Tom and Pam bought. An old sea captain once owned the property which was the site of his farm in the 1800's. The property had stayed in the family since. In recent years, the small cottage has been updated and used as a vacation retreat after the family moved from the area. When we first viewed its interior, old photos of the captain's sailing ship were on the walls (now gone with the rest of the family furnishings). Situated on a small road, which includes the lane past Carol and Ken's home and several other cottages is called Cap's Lane, and is now part of Tom and Pam's domain; however, it is semi-maintained by the Road Comm. Tom, who loves all things nautical, is understandably elated. He is hoping to obtain a copy of the old schooner photo from Capt Simonsen's family. Jo

06.6.16   Mothers' Day

Burba, Mother's Day satisfied every mother's expectations . . . . I had 14 children and grandchildren at the table. Was fun to have Abby home with a friend from Venezuela who enjoyed all the people and confusion, claiming there are nearly 50 present for his family occasions. (I know Earl will ask if this was a family or a cartel.) Since I had picked rhubarb last week, we had rhubarb cake, rhubarb pies, and everyone went home with a jar of rhubarb jam. So much for this week's crop. Love, jojo

6.20.06

Have grandchildren checked for rhubarb fever.
Love, BoBB

06.7.4   Rum Cake and Tears

Burba, I was thinking about you last evening as you served up your world class tetrazzini to all those really nice people seated at your candlelit tables strewn with small seashells. I daydreamed of walking in the door, full of interesting stories from the north, dressed somewhat like a Chicos ad, to do real damage to the miniature key lime pie count. I came back to earth in time to take the weekend "monster goulash" (hard to find good monsters these days) from the oven, and mix up another batch of Hawaiian Punch. But, my table, too, seated very nice people. The beginning of the 4th of July fun for my family.

I wanted to tell you about worship in our little church this morning. You are so close to the military at all times in Beaufort, and see your "boys" take to the skies daily. All of us have feelings about warfare, but they are never so deep as when we have our arms around someone who leaves for a war zone. My dear friends, Dick and Eleanor Weycker, were in church this morning with their entire family which included their son Will, his wife and children. Will is an army Capt., going back for his second tour in Iraq, a very dangerous post, as you know. Trinity held its annual 4th of July service; and my pal Annie, a gifted concert pianist in an earlier time, provided full organ accompaniment to *Battle Hymn of the Republic, America the Beautiful, God Bless America* and *The National Anthem* during the service. She told me last week she planned to play *The Caissons Go Rolling* . . . for the offertory. But, by that time, in an emotional turmoil of patriotism and sadness, I had to keep coughing like I was getting a cold so that I could keep wiping my nose and eyes. At the little social after service, Will reminded me to keep his Mom honest about her golf score, and therefore I had an opportunity to reassure him that his entire family would be sheltered and reinforced by the Stonington community. Then we had our hug, and I had to cough again. There was a cake on the table for Will, generously laced with rum in a very un-Lutheran way. Delicious . . . . but, until Will and all our troops are home safely, I believe I will have this sadness on the 4th of July when I hear all the patriotic music, and I will taste rum cake and tears. love from jojo and fcwss

06.8.9   FAARPs, et al.

Burba, This past weekend's deck party is now old news, and my houseguest and bed partner, Breeze the Beast, has returned to her own family. Consider 10 dinner guests hydrating in the heat with vodka and tonics and a beast in the kitchen trailing MilkBone crumbs or lounging on the new duvet farting away the Pupperoni treats. Monday, however, dear friend Ace and I had a "play day" which included golf, big whitefish sandwiches and beer, visiting a new gift shop, the casino (where Avis actually won money and I only observed like some pit boss). Then we shared a Big Turtle Sundae which, thankfully, was not a Native American specialty but simply an ice cream dessert.

Speaking of whitefish, last week we Friends And Associates of Rich People (the FAARPs) drove over to the Nahma Hotel, located part way to Manistique, for dinner. We were served whitefish so fresh that we saw fishermen carrying them into the kitchen! You gotta love the U.P. Today, I had to weigh in at the doctor's for a final check on the tick-related infection where I learned the tick died in vain and I am cured. jojo and fishcalledwandasandyspike

06.8.14   Blowing Up The Bridge, Kitchen Cabinetry

Burba, I Turned on the news this a.m. for happy reports on the weather, and learned there was a group who had planned to blow up the Mackinac Bridge. No . . . not some Yoopers who have tired of the summer tourists and their endless caravans of campers and rv's . . . . but three Detroit "radical fundamentalists." Don't these bombers know Upper Michigan is God's Country??? Anyhoo, (one of my favorite words from "Fargo") the plan is already forming in local bars whereby the little weasels are forwarded to the U.P. for sentencing . . . . something that involves hunting season and a running start.

I have a new carpenter working on the kitchen project, and if he were 35 years older and owned a golf cart, I would be in love. He has taken charge of the whole project, incorporating very good ideas and scrapping some of my budget-busting redo in exchange for better, more practical changes. He is so cheerful and charming in his shirts with environmental reminders and his old hiking boots. I've settled for feeding him like a grandson and making sure I have enough money to pay him. jj and fcwss

06.9.6   Grandgirls Gone

BBOFB, I'm hoping the worst of Hurricane Ernesto is well beyond you by now. I have been thinking of you parked in the high country next to an electrical hookup and beer depot. I've seen your evacuation checklist, remember.

Our warm, sunny weather continues. Knowing what is coming soon, (NOTE: All Yoopers know the signs . . . unusual abundance of acorns on the ground, the matted cedars and really wooly woolyworms . . . warnings to all critters who linger here that the winter will be a hard one) there was a great flurry of activity yesterday all along the shoreline. Everyone pulling in the docks, shore stations and, in our case, the lift for the jetski. The beach umbrellas are stored in the garden shed, and the vintage lounges have been folded and shoved up into the garage rafters. The grandgirls who lay upon them whispering and giggling to each other in the sun have all gone away and taken our summer with them. love from jojo and fishcalledwandasandyspike

06.9.9   Letter to France

Steve and Claudia,

Very chilly this morning. Frost in many areas. I awoke to the sound of the furnace chugging away at the oil reserves. And so, thank you for the wonderful letter taking me to the vineyards in France where the vintage excitement is building. All seasonal things here have been stored away. Molly is fitting in beautifully at the University of

Michigan; Abby is back at Michigan Tech: AmyJo at Bay College before moving on to (perhaps) Lake Superior State University; Ryan in his last undergraduate year at Northern Michigan University; and our Kellee Kaboose playing soccer with her daddy as coach . . . Go Purple Pirates!! I miss them. But, have occupied myself with the kitchen redo. My carpenter is doing the final kitchen work, during which time I am supposed to hostess the Stonington Ladies Card Club. This could be good . . . I will not have to clean my house, telling the ladies that, as they will be able to see, I am in the midst of a Mess. I could point out the missing sink and stove, with great apologies for the lack of a fantastic dessert. Brilliant!!. I hear you are planning to spend time here next summer; and I look forward to seeing you then, and, especially, to hearing your travel stories first-hand, Claudia. I will, in turn, try to entertain you with my collection of taped Gilles Marini appearances on "Dancing with the Stars" . . . a real incentive to board my pet fish and fly to meet you in France. Nothing lovelier than a real Frenchman who has mastered salsa. love from jojo

06.9.12   Tumbling Tumbleweeds

BBofB, I visited with Kim and family in Longmont, CO, a beautiful neighborhood abutting Boulder. The recent addition to their house features a second story room with a wall of windows facing Long Mt., one of the 14,000 ft. peaks in the range. I believe we have a fascination for things we fear . . . and being a card-carrying acrophobic, (I think that's a person who doesn't enjoy high places and screams in elevators) I could look out at the mountains endlessly. The Denver kids are vegetarians; thus, near the end of my stay, the lack of beef (Remember! I am the butcher's daughter, raised on steaks and nourishing pot roasts) was responsible for the best story of that visit. Celebrating Kim's birthday and my last night in town, we went out for dinner at Tres Margaritas where I had non margaritas, but the biggest platter of sizzling beef on the menu. On a high from the beef, I then sang with the strolling, singing cowboy, who, along with everyone in the cantina . . . except Kim and the rest of our party (who were spending a long time in the restrooms) . . . was astonished that I knew every, single word in three verses of "Cool Water." The cowboy asked me to go on the road with him. I also know all the words to every verse of "Tumbling Tumbleweeds" but will keep that a surprise for my next visit . . . . Love, jojo

06.10.1   Abby in the Duck Blind

BBof B, This morning I had the best treat. It is opening day of duck season; and at daylight I looked out toward the little blind Jeff has built on the edge of my beach. Two heads in there bent toward each other in conversation. Abby hunting with her Daddy. How wonderful that was! I remember my Dad taking me out to his duck blind in front of the old cabin on Bay Mills, and the two of us in a little world of dried reeds and cattails talking away about everything, waiting for the sun to rise. If I was hungry, he would pull a sandwich out of one of the big pockets in his hunting jacket. He was German, you recall, so the bread was thickly sliced and the liberal spread of butter held the big slices of sausage he loved. These sandwiches he prepared himself and neatly wrapped in waxed paper. No breakfast has tasted as delicious since. And later,

Weather nasty . . . . This steady drizzle will soon turn to snow. The transient geese and mallards at my shoreline are enjoying some sort of convention all around Jeff's empty duck blind, their agenda unaffected by the weather. This news I do not share with Jeff who daily asks me if I see any ducks on the bay. Since he is unable to be out there hunting them, I spare him disappointment by confining my bird watching reports to rare swan sightings. jj

O6.9.21   Warming up the World

BBofB, Friend Sparky (Ann) and I are co-chairmen of our FCE "Warm Up The World" project, which we immediately relabeled the "Warm Up Delta County" project. As a co-chairman, I am entrusted with the grant money to keep everyone supplied with the yarn, knitting needles and crochet hooks needed to complete warm, colorful afghans. As with all grants, I learned that the money must be spent within the allotted time . . . . ALL OF IT . . . or you might go on some sort of blacklist at Grant Headquarters, and never again see easy money. I am going crazy trying to spend ALL OF IT. I go out of the store with two shopping baskets of yarn, finding I have bought so much that they have given me a big discount and I have a fortune left over. I make another shopping trip, this time to Marquette, to load up with the discount windfall, only to learn at the checkout, the order is so large, they are treating me as if I were four customers, and allowing me a 20% discount plus a rebate because I am an organization. I now have so much yarn stockpiled in my garage I may have to park my car outside . . . and I have money. But, thanks to the wonderful ladies of this group, Sparky and I are exceeding our most hopeful expectations for this project. We have begun rolling up the afghans, tying each with grosgraine ribbon. These will be distributed by St. Vincent de Paul and the Salvation Army at Christmas, at which time we will have used up even the skeins of clearance priced fushia in the corner of the garage. With all these shopping trips and meetings, I leave the house telling my carpenter I am off to do community service, leading him to think I am a felon on probation.

love from jojo and fishcalledwandasandyaspike

Chairman JoJo , , , I gave some thought to the grant money and cannot see you getting out of your current situation unless you try embezzlement. Fill that old car up with gas for the trips to the yarn store; don't you need lunch and some entertainment for all these wonderful people who give you such

deals? How about rent on the storage building
where the yarn is stored? Money for your
Granddaughter to tell you what the latest
afghan colors are in Ann Arbor. Go for it,
Jo, and SPEND. That is what government is all
about. Love, Burba

P.S. You are slowing up wheel chairs with the
knitted strips.

06.10.18   Dort

Dorothy Anne Rood was the big sister I had always wished for while
growing up. We became friends when she took the job as office
manager for the law firm where I was employed. In my darkest and
most frightening times Dort always managed to be there. For years
I carried a key to their house she had made for me, and Roods' door
was the one I went to the night I began a new life. Through the chaos
of my daily life at times, she quietly went about making sure I was
not alone; and when times were good, we did all the things that
friends do together . . . shopping trips, long walks around her home
at Indian Lake, exchanged books and recipes and notes full of news
of the grandchildren. When her husband died a few years ago, not
even her family or the countless people who loved her could restore
her spirit. By then illness had begun to take its toll, and she moved
from Indian Lake to her daughter's home in Manistique. I would
drive over to spend an occasional morning or afternoon with her, the
two of us chatting away, surrounded by her veterinarian daughter's
cats, dogs and birds. Sometime after we had become friends, we
learned we were Sigma Kappa sorority sisters who had attended
different schools. So we always had our little joke about "sigma
news" which had escaped us, and tried to find little gifts emblazoned
with violets , , , the sorority flower. When I last visited her, we sat
together without words, as old friends can, held hands and looked

into each other's face for the final time. I feel such loss, and I grieve. But, Oh, how blessed I was to have had her to enrich my life and to leave me joy in the remembering.

P.S. to this story. Several months after Dort's death, her daughter came to visit, bringing her mother's Sigma Kappa pin. She said that when it was found in Dort's jewelry box, she knew immediately where the pin belonged. About this time, my granddaughter, Molly, pledged Sigma Kappa at the U of M and I planned to be at her induction ceremony and put my pin on her. This I did, while wearing my last gift from Dort. As Molly would say . . . "mystic bond."

06.11.1   Delta Zeta Disguise

Burba, Am packing up for my trip to Ann Arbor. This is the weekend of Molly's Sigma Kappa initiation, and I pass my pin to her. The initiation is Sunday a.m. (can't interfere with Saturday's football schedule), followed by brunch. I will show up at the house in my long white dress, clutching my yellowed initiation certificate (which they think may have historical value by now), trying not to look like a security risk . . . or worse, a Delta Zeta in disguise. Looking forward to the ceremony and traditions, Molly's new sisters, etc. Worrying about the long white dress which I let out three inches and makes me look like I have historical value. This is about Molly, however, and she says she is excited to have her gramma with her. Will send you a photo . . . jo

November 6, 2006

Jo, What a deal, you actually have a long white dress? That is amazing even with it three inches out of size. I do not think that I ever had a long white dress so it is a good thing that I pledged a different Sorority.

```
Hoping   your   trip   was   the   very   best.   Love,
Barbara
```

06.11.06

Moll Doll,

It was dark by the time your Mom and I reached the Mackinac Bridge and . . . . Lo!!! all the spans on the bridge were lit with Christmas lights!! With the full moon coming up and all the colorful lights, it was quite a beautiful show. We stopped briefly at McDonalds for our senior 60 cent cup of coffee and kept on going. We were still full of our lunch from Whole Foods in Ann Arbor (together with a few rumblings from the previous evening's Thai meal). Laurie and I never run out of things to talk about; and we gave that a break by singing with my CD of 70's hits and calling Jeff periodically to reassure him that we were indeed still alright and on schedule. He wanted a description of every little detail of seeing you and how your initiation went. Mostly, I can read into all this that he wants to make sure you are happy and secure. And I tell him that you are where you should be . . . it is all such a good fit for you. How lovely you looked, Molly, and how sweet you remain. Stay as you are . . . . honest and open and kind and caring. New experiences and diverse friends are enriching . . . . enjoy them for that. Never change yourself to have new experiences or to make friends. Okay . . . well, I have hung the sorority dress in the closet, and am back in my old grey sweats moving wood this morning. I am myself . . . but I truly enjoyed my time back with all the little Sisters, and am feeling so proud of our newest Sigma, who is also my Granddaughter. Really . . . we should write a song . . . . very much love, gramma

p.s. Yesterday I drove over to Garden to a tea prepared by the Kate's Bay group in our Family and Community Education Association. (heretofore and after referred to as FCE) Remember, this organization started as little groups of home extension ladies in rural areas who met to enhance their roles as homemakers. Cooking, sewing, etc. were the earliest projects of these extension groups, sponsored and nourished by Michigan State University . . . . skills that remain obvious within the organization. The "tea" was a feast of homemade hot dishes and salads, pies, cakes, and trays of fudge and candies. A small auction was held where we could bid on lovely little items from attics and cellars, as well as beautiful jars of canned fruits and jams from Kates' Bay kitchens, tied in Christmas ribbons. We will open a quart of picture perfect, plump peaches on Christmas Day for our brunch when you all come to Stonington. G.

06.11.20   Curves Coupons

BBofB, Tuesday I wore a costume to Curves for the promise of extra Curves dollars (little slips of paper you can trade for their merchandise). I'm saving my coupons for a workout shirt, which I will wear to . . . . you guessed it . . . Curves. I'm beginning to wonder if their program is more an altered mental state than exercise. Seriously, I really like it (see, I'm already altered!). The kitchen project is 85% complete by my estimate . . . 100% by the carpenter's. His work is done and I must take over with the finish work now. I have a new stove which I thought really spiffy because it was all black. Now I find I have to DUST it off because everything shows up. Don't even think about what happens when I cook my beloved fried hamburgers. Today the sun is warming things up enough that I may be able to give the windows one last good washing before I have to peer through the grime until May. All is well here . . . but I feel as if we are poised on the edge of a calm, waiting for the blowing snow to come bearing down upon us. After reading the last line, I close to go to the closet and haul out my special winter lamp to sit under and raise my endorphins. love from, jojo and fishcalledwandasandyspike

06.11.30   Wrapping Up at the Meat Plant

Burba, I finished wrapping venison at Michigan Meats yesterday. This will probably be the last deer season here for me. About time I retire from this job after working my way up through the years to part-time seasonal work! As I write, my work clothes are going through the "TOXIC-HEAVY WASH-STERLIZE-DEODORIZE'" cycle for the last time this year. I will tend to picking the meat scraps out of my boot cleats later. For weeks I will not succumb to grocer ads for beef or pork, and will hunger only for fresh fish. Even the bottom—of—the—freezer shrimp at Elmer's will seem tasty. I will always and forever regard hamburger with suspicion. Because I am as close as you get to being employee of the month at a meat plant, my boss took me out for a tour of the huge new plant under construction. I got to see the "bad place" where the animals come in . . . . probably thinking they have won a weekend at Applegate Farms. One cooler will hold 180 sides of beef. The front of the complex will have a retail store to market meats, their very excellent sausages and specialty items. Todd and some of the Neomokong hunters are partial to the venison bacon "we" produce. I am happy for this family enterprise. They work constantly to expand and reinvent a strenuous business, and I'm pleased they treat me as part of their November household. Every time I put on my boots and apron, I think of how hard my dad worked in this business and the nice home on Hursley, all the prom dresses and college . . . .

07.3.5   Letter to Al Gore

Burba, As I write, Mother Nature continues blasting Stonington and the entire "Upper Great Lakes Region" * with a raging blizzard in response to all those hardened Yoopers who yammer about how mild the winter has been, and to please the pansies who fled to Alabama with their Social Security raise. The only good thing about the howling around my house is the happy thought that we are somehow disappointing Al Gore. We have had abundant weather advisories for the past week, allowing school kids and teachers to make fun plans for the expected closings, and leaving me to cancel mine, erasing, one by one, those happy little scratches I had on my fresh and hopeful March calendar. I ventured out early yesterday to shovel a path to the garage. I lost footing on the buried step only to find myself face and mittens first in a snow mountain off the deck, thus creating the area's largest natural ice cave. I went back inside to my fire and my books. Later, in my pressed and brushed Lutheran funeral suit, I set off for a memorial service in town . . . and buried my brave little Honda in the snow mountain which by now had drifted from near the deck to 400 feet down Twin Springs Lane. I tried the usual exertions we Yoopers practice to free ourselves: shoveling, cursing, rocking, cursing. These efforts only sweated up my funeral suit, plastered my fresh hairdo to the back of my head and filled my semi-dress boots with wet snow. A real hero with Red Wings stickers and a plow on his truck came along and rescued me. I backed up to my house and went inside to the fire, my books and the emergency bottle of Scotch . . . with which I toasted the departed friend we were to memorialize in a more Lutheran manner. And after, I thought of you shopping in a cotton shirt at Hilton Head and MaryEllen polishing up the little beads on her dancing dress for the Miles Grand President's Ball. However, each day the sun is higher and soon it will be spring, and with that thought, also, I remember my friend with stage IV cancer. Thinking of her and others makes me grateful that I am still able to fall into snowbanks, get up and look forward to spring while laughing at global warming. Love from jojo *Upper Great Lakes Region: (The Arctic Circle usually included in this designation by the weather lady's sweeping finger)

```
To: Al Gore

Somewhere on another planet

Dear Al Baby:

I am enclosing a letter from my friend in Rapid
River regarding global warming. She is 73 years
old, and needs some help with her shoveling
and getting to memorial services (not her own)
in one piece, so I would appreciate it if you
could warm up northern Michigan, including the
ski areas where it has been too cold for my
grandchildren to ski at $65 a throw. I would
go out on my porch and smoke some cigarettes
if that might help my friend get off the Scotch
without rehab. Best wishes from South Carolina
where you only got one vote and it sure wasn't
mine. Burba of Beautiful Beaufort
```

07.3.27   Planes, Planes, Automobiles

Burba, Thanks for the call just before I lapsed into a coma. How nice to hear your voices as I drifted off! The trip went well, but there seemed like a lot of hopping out of cars and aircraft and a looooonnnngggg wait in the Detroit terminal ("tunnel music") before embarking on the last leg of the trip. The final 45 minutes to home provided all the thrills aviation has to offer; and I learned some Shinto prayers from the little Japanese couple across the aisle (who were going to Ishpeming (??????). I see I have a $300 bill for furnace repairs. I went south so I wouldn't have to listen to the furnace running. I never thought it would just quit without me. Such devotion. Jeff is spending his evenings remodeling the basement into a family room-gathering place for hordes of teenieboppers now hanging out in the kitchen and living room. Was our life that exciting?? I only remember you and Donald nearly burning the house down one night with a cozy fire on the hearth.

07.4.12   Snow Plow Thief

Earl, The daily winter storm advisory has been lifted, but it is still snowing on Stonington. The local tv newscaster advises that this morning a county snowplow was hijacked near the Wisconsin border. We are assuming it will be easy to spot. It is large and orange and presumed heading south. I know how that guy feels. This probably is funny to people in kinder climates who are stealing convertibles; but, right now, in the U.P. we can only feel great empathy with the plow thief and worry over one less plow!! love from the Smelt Goddess

07.4.15   Smelt Goddess Takes a Dive

Hi Jo, I was pleased to see that Al finally sent you the weather you asked for. I do not think his intention was for you you to hit golf balls onto passing icebergs. The idea was to stretch out a lovely bunch of clothes lines across your yard and stop using the dryer. In fact, he would prefer you took in the neighbors' sheets and washed them in cold water (no soap). So if you are hotter than hell this summer, do not blame me. In fact, we are getting worried. It is already very summery here in SC.

And . . . . ¾ of a pound is a lot to lose. Grab up a big lump of hamburger next time you are at Elmer's and plop it on your boobs. It will nearly knock you over into the freezer atop the frozen smelt. What a headline for the local paper!! "Smelt Goddess Takes a Dive While Placing Frozen Burger on Her Soo Hi Sweatshirt." Love, BofBB

07.9.30   Fluffing Up the Old Fleece, The Economy

Burba, Weather turning quickly here, and I'm scrambling to save
the windowbox plants I promised a winter in the house. My shabby
fleece wardrobe is looking good again, and this weekend I will do a
roast in the oven. The State of Michigan is facing bankruptcy (big
deal . . . I've skirted this for years!); UofM's first two games have
caused more alarm than the state's bankruptcy, and we are two days
into bear season. I call the grandchildren to ask "How's School?" . . .
the standard ice-breaker used by generations. Now I hear tales of Calc
3; International Marketing; Organic Chemistry. Am supposing I won't
have any papers for my refrigerator door again this semester. Today
I will drive to town in search of a new crockpot. I used my former
pot melting wax during my candle-making phase. Thank you for the
comforting card after the death of fishcalledwandasandyspike. That
little empty space in our hearts and on the bookcase (non-fiction
section) has been filled by a new and eerily similar beta.

The annual Stonington BIG RUMMAGE SALE is set for Saturday
in the field adjacent to the township hall. I will move the aforesaid
bankruptcy further off by selling items from my garage that I'm certain
everyone (except me) can't live without beyond Saturday; i.e., a door,
poker table, colorful garden hose, patio umbrella, etc., if, that is,
I don't see things on sale I can't live without beyond Saturday. Stay
tuned. love, jojo and fishcalledwandasandythesecond

P.S. We U.P. Packer fans are so high on Brett Favre, beer and onion dip
we barely noticed that the Gov. and Leg. struck a deal Monday a.m.
to ward off bankruptcy, filling a $1.75 billion shortfall by raising our
state income tax from 3.9% to 4.35% . . . and our 6% sales tax will be
expanded to cover 53 service categories. Newly taxed services include
ski lift fees, a good example of how raising taxes eventually depresses
the economy. I caught an interview with the manager of one of the ski
resorts up here (Marquette) who claims a lift ticket will go up to $42 a
day . . . a price which will limit the number of trips families will make
to the ski hill. I also noted on the list of income-generating taxables,

"Bronzing Baby Shoes." This last item would border on humorous if we didn't have to picture all those sad little empty spots on Michigan bookshelves in the future because new families must economize, choosing benefits for their children's teachers over having their (the children's) shoes bronzed.

Color at its peak in this area, but weather remains in the 70's. I took a drive to Marquette yesterday to enjoy the color and shop for a new winter jacket. Things you don't see in SC: miles of red and gold birch and maple accented by stands of blue spruce, as well as racks of puffy Woolrich jackets with matching boiled wool caps.

07.10.7

Jo, It is so completely sad!! I have an idea to help out the State of Michigan. Stop advertising on cable TV to "Bring your company to Michigan." This would allow everyone to get the baby shoes taken care of (do babies still wear shoes??) because NO one is going to bring their company anywhere near Michigan for fear bankruptcy might be catching. Your example of the ski tickets was excellent. Kathy's employees are not worried about the higher income tax because they are mostly laid off.

I am so excited about the game tonight, but Earl is worried Green Bay might win again, and leaving our Packer flag up week after week is fading it. He keeps making appointments to have it drycleaned and special unguents applied. Oh, Brett, that fox, has confounded all but the diehard crowd. Wish I could spend tonight at the Broke Spoke. And wish you and I could watch the game together. DO NOT GIVE THE FISH LEFTOVER ONION DIP!!. Love to the UP from BofBB

07.10.15   Conserving Energy

BBofB, The bay breezes are filled with dead leaves. I have given up raking and will get busy preparing for the next phase of our weather cycle . . . inspecting the weather stripping, stacking wood and checking on my subscription to "Islands" magazine. I attended an energy conservation program at the township hall yesterday afternoon and picked up some ideas. The offer of free CF lightbulbs, new ballpoint pens and refreshments is always a draw for us Stoningtonites.

I am looking after anniecat this week while DJ travels. I drop by his house to feed and water her, and we sit together for a while and talk about old times. She is doing beautifully there. Has the entire heated basement to enjoy, prescription cat food and scented litter. Also she is groomed regularly (by a groomer who must have terrible scars by now). When I see her, I go away missing her, but try not to show this to fishcalledwandasandythesecond who has a fragile ego. jojo

08.2.15   Travel Tales

BBofB, I came back too soon. Caught a "cold" as temperatures bottomed out at—33 degrees somewhere off the coast of Lake Superior. My usual remedies (one part brandy, 3 parts nap under the puffy quilt) failed, leaving me voiceless, short-winded and feeling old and sick. I could handle the laryngitis and less lung power, but the last two issues worried me. I picked the feathers out of my hair, washed off one coat of VapoRub and consulted a doctor. She prescribed antibiotics and less Fox News. I'm recovering, but due to the rampant and severe flu in the U.P., I am suffering from lack of human contact. My best friends have left cartons of soup and little bags of fresh fruit and cookies inside my storm door, but are already speeding out the driveway before my quilt and I can make it down the hallway.

I had the fun of "bonding" with Scott and Don's Dobermans this trip. They went from regarding me as an interesting snack to an entertainment of sorts. They sat and listened quietlyas I told them stories of the woods at grandma's where chipmunks live. Cole and Pepper are full grown and fearsome. The attention they paid to my voice and the words it produced was an experience. Their eyes are black and bottomless, unsettling because they watch so intently. But both sat there as if children at a story hour, and behind those eyes they were cataloging the happy part of having a grandma. Scott tells me that they miss me and seem to expect my return. He also said that the word "chipmunk" cannot be said because they become either animated at the wonderful word or depressed because there is no grandma to tell the story.

MaryEllen and I had a few days in Stuart to engage in our usual craziness before she and her friend drove me to West Palm Beach, dropping me off at the Amtrak station and hurrying off to shop upscale. As the train approached, the porter discovered my suitcase was now 3 pounds over the limit with overused clothes and books. Nothing would satisfy the Railroad but to lighten the load to the approved weight. (I tried bribery, waving my AARP card, etc.) I was asked to go back to the ticket agent and acquire "an approved container" . . . which turned out to be a black plastic garbage bag. So as the train was rolling into the station, I was exposing my old K-Mart undies and CareBear nightshirt to the ladies of Palm Beach as I threw the forbidden overage into an approved carry-on. If there was any suspicion in Florida that I might be a secret Yooper, boarding a train carrying clothes in a garbage bag was a real giveaway. love, jojo

08.4.1 Make a Wish

Burba,

Whatever disaster you are seeing on your Upper Michigan weather map is real. We have been under a "winter storm" advisory since yesterday morning. The promised storm moved into Stonington about suppertime last evening, and we have had 45 mph wind from the north, sleet, heavy snow, thunder and lightning. I have been feeding Lorna Doones to a sorry little raccoon who is hunkered down by the corner of my deck, just away from the squirrels who are gratefully nibbling on soggy apple peelings I've salvaged for them from the garbage basket. Look for me and starving little forest creatures on a segment of Planet Earth about global warming.

But . . . I had a phone call this a.m. (other than the one from my neighbor to tell me a semi was jackknifed near Rapid River and the road was closed). The caller said they were calling for some sort of "make a wish" foundation. I shouted: "Thank God . . . . ! My wish is to go back to South Carolina!" There was a silence then a dial tone. I guess I don't get the wish. love, jojo

08.5.15   Lettuce Seeds

Burba, Spring has forgotten about the Upper Peninsula. It has skipped over us, making stops in Green Bay and Oconto, Wisconsin before traveling through here late one night to somewhere east of Lake Ontario. The endangered polar bears are gathering for a mass migration to this area where global warming is not a threat. I persevere, and standing in my swampers, plant the first lettuce seeds for the rabbits' garden. In my quilted jacket I trudge up the frosted greens at Gladstone with feet in thermal socks stuffed into my golf shoes. They are selling Heet in the pro shop for the golf carts. Will we go directly from winter to tick season? And I could have been in Charleston this weekend with the kids. I haven't heard from them, and am thinking they may have inherited guilt from their gramma jojo and don't want me know what I'm missing. Hope you are bracing yourself for July and all those reminders of our 75th birthdays, which happy wishes usually come from younger people. Meanwhile, let's live it up while we are still young and 74. Love, jojo and fishcalledwandasandythesecond

08.11.21   Snow Raking

Dear Tom, Jeff, Kim and Scott,

Yooper is an authentic civilization. Having a documented culture, we are entitled to our own unique customs, costumes and ethnic cuisine, said cuisine including . . . and tied for #1 with venison stew . . . Grilled Bratwurst. We have no freeway smog in the Upper Peninsula of Michigan, no noxious factory fumes or lingering miasma suffered by uncaring and more wasteful civilizations.

What we have from early spring until first serious snowfall is a thin, richly scented mist from thousands of outdoor grills roasting up bratwurst. Some hardy Yoopers extend the outdoor grilling season by cooking in a shoveled out area on the deck or just inside the open garage door (at a safe distance, mostly, from the family car and/or lawnmower). Grilling outdoors in winter takes special, warmly clad volunteers who must stand in swampers at the grill, keeping their attention to the task while stealing looks through the frosted windows at happy family and friends sitting by the fire.

I now reluctantly store the old Weber as the last leaves from the oaks begin to freeze in the eave gutters. I've had no complaints about this deadline from those who have taken their turn keeping the brats from burning when the temperature is below zero. But, the grill is the final item to go into the garden shed . . . after the beach chairs, after the wind chimes and deck planters, after the canoe paddles and tiki torches . . ., to keep company with the big and little water shoes. It is the last piece of summer left to store, and so I put off removing from view this definitive reminder of warm, happy days here on the Bay.

Today's writing is about waiting too long. As the wind from the NE became ominous last week, and random snowflakes reached us from Marquette, I went out and, after emptying leftover ashes into the woods, wheeled the Weber into storage. Late in the day, I stood looking out the window as I washed up the dishes, and spied its broiling rack on the ground where it had been laid . . . then forgot it until the random snowflakes turned to serious lake effect snow yesterday, leaving my grill's innards buried. Here is a perfect situation for Yooper ingenuity, a gift of our aforesaid culture. I'm off now to seek out the garden rake and, in the howling wind, will dig around the disappearing lakeside yard. This entry is for my children in case the neighbors call to tell them their mother is out raking the snow.

Love, Mom

09.3.13   Sweet Burba From Pike

Jo: Been in Texas for a week. Have never seen the sun. Up in the mountains in a desert area. It rans everyday. Tonight maybe snow. Deep mud. First we threw away the bedspread and a décor pillow. After a conversation, we tossed the dirty sheets. Wish I had a piano to leave by the side of the road. Love, Pioneer Woman

Dear Sweet Burba From Pike (who crossed the wide mountains with her husband Earl), How did I happen to recall that old 3rd grade song? Remember the little music books we sang from during "music time?" The first song therein: "Old Folks At Home" which I thought a misnomer for years because we called it "Swanee River" . . . Let me know where to send spokes for the wheels or another barrel of flour. Glad to know you left your piano back at home. Would be so sad to see it used for firewood above the timberline.

The temperature (after weeks of subzero) is supposed to climb to 10 degrees today. This is perhaps the result of my "sun dance" performed on the black ice of the sidewalk in the snow tunnel to my garage while wearing the traditional Yooper "sun dance" costume of 4 layers of jackets and pants, blaze orange knit cap, Soo Woolen Mills socks and swampers. It has taken six weeks for my dance to actually work, but the exercise keeps me from freezing before I reach the garage. I heard news reports of citizens succumbing to the subzero temps after walking down the road. Perhaps they will find me someday in a snowbank with a map of South Carolina clutched in my frozen fingers . . . with one thumb pointing South. jojo

09.3.28   Menards Opening

BBofB, Tell Earl the "all you can eat" smelt fries are everywhere now, and the smoke from the fryers all over the U.P. is contributing to global greasing. Bring it on!!! Smelt Goddess

P.S. The new really big Menards opened in Escanaba last week. It was a great social event. We all made our plans to drive over and mill around the dazzling electrical and plumbing sections where we ran into people we haven't seen since Fall. Old friendships were renewed, new attachments were formed, divorcees reconciled, and one do-it-yourself couple was married in the model kitchen. I had a good conversation with an interesting man choosing lightbulbs. I noticed he wasn't buying those squiggly bulbs that force you to read in dim light, a plus in my eligibility ratings. We both bought soon-to-be-extinct 75 watt soft lights. We really hit it off. Perhaps we'll meet again over the free coffee and eats at the Grand Opening scheduled for a later date. Stay tuned. jojo

09.3.31

JoJo: Did I not spend half my life in Menards? How lucky of you to hit one of their Grand Openings! You should have asked the light bulb man what wattage his wife preferred.

09.8.3   Wedding Preparations

Burba, 17 more days until the children, partners, sister, assorted animals arrive for Abby and Justin's wedding. I have secured all the sleeping arrangements, thanks to the neighbors next door. This leaves me to finish small projects like fresh gravel in the driveway and having my tv service "split" to afford more than one dim tv in the household. I have completed washing up the bar glasses for the Miami/Ft. Lauderdale boys and stocked up on BocaBurgers for the Denver branch. Finishing up the beach project, I hauled flat rock in the trunk of my Honda from the waters off Tommy's place and placed them along the sidewalk to my beach, which will keep the grass from infringing on the newly edged sidewalk. While planting marked down WalMart shrubs on my hands and knees (taking advantage of this position because I couldn't straighten up after laying the rock), I came to a practical decision . . . . I will alter my search for the perfect man. I am thinking along the lines of a Russian olympic weightlifter. I now find a strong back very sexy in a man. The language might be a problem, but I could invest in a "Conversational Russian" course with the money I save on a chiropractor. I'm off to town with hopes there will be some of the pink frosted cookies shaped like a penis left over from Abby's bachelorette party. love, jojo

09.8.25   Abby and Justin's Wedding

BBofB, The wedding is a wonderful memory. Abby, born beautiful, brought all her loveliness to that day. A mother watches her child in a small moment, and because of the years of love and awareness that have gone before, her heart feels his emotion so deeply. Jeff giving his Abby that little kiss at the end of the aisle and stepping away. I am so proud of him and Laurie. They raised their daughters with such love and respect that they absolutely get the whole thing about family. Abby and Justin were one of those rare couples who appeared to be having a good time at their own wedding. Molly was a great maid of honor, rallying everyone when it was time to toast, dance, eat more cake, or whatever was required for a proper tribute to her sister. I did my best with my now (in)famous "hamster" dance, performed in my painfully new dressy shoes. I then sedately celebrated from the comfort of my chair near the dessert table. After a honeymoon, the newlyweds will be back to their work and studies at Michigan Tech. For one day, every one of my children, grandchildren and great grandson were in my house at the same time; and the next day they were all gone at once. As you well know, these moments with the family are precious indeed . . . and I had a dance with my son, Jeff. I have a photo to prove it. We look happy. jojo

09.11.19   Some Kind of Goo Be Gone

BBofB, I have worn my Cabela's jacket since the Alaska trip in 1997 with dribbles of dried caulking I had used to seal the log beams under my roof. My favorite and most necessary piece of clothing, I had tried all the recommended methods to remove the patches which made it look like my "dinner" ("breakfast" and/or "lunch") jacket. A call to Cabelas confirmed that the jacket might wear out before the caulking wore off. Remember the frozen well problem that was solved at the Lutheran church coffee hour? The kinship of Stonington reaches out to remove stains from your jacket. Stopping off at our Stonington Mall (Bob and Jeanie's Garth Bluff Grocery/Beer and Wine/Hunting-Fishing Licenses/Ice Dispenser/Bottled Gas Supply/ Deer Feed Center) for that extra carton of milk and the weekly lottery ticket, I added Bob to the list of people who had heard my explanation of the spotted jacket. He whipped out a bottle of Some Kinda Goo B Gone from under the counter and sprayed me in exchange for a plate of brownies I was going home to bake. I am now spot free and further convinced that this has to be the best place ever to live , , , especially for people like myself who just always need help. Jojo

09.12.23   To Hell and Back

BBofB, I've been to hell and back on my lunch hour. I drove over to WalMart on the day before the day before Christmas. The last minute shopping demons were there waiting for me. Lining up their carts two abreast in aisle 4, they defended the sale-priced cranberry sauce. They had bought up every ingredient for my Christmas Kiss cookies. They left me only mushy avocados, their fingerprints still imprinted on the shriveled peels. All remaining pineapples were green, and the pears will not ripen until Groundhog Day. Shoving ahead of me they pushed their overflowing carts into the "20 Or Less Items" line. The checkout clerk's stapler malfunctioned, so he took a break just as my green pineapple reached his scanner. Finally, fighting my way to the exit, I stood in the slush trying to remember where I had left my car . . . somewhere between the gates of hell and Ludington Park. hoho from jojo

10.6.3   Frank Yerby Books

BBofB, Yes, I remember our earliest "reading." My (always hopeful) parents enrolled me in the Junior Literary Guild at a very young age which provided me with the best kind of stories. Many of these early books have been passed on to the grandchildren. However, even before the teen years, you and I were sneaking Frank Yerby novels home from the library under the disapproving notice of the librarian. She still remembered this when I saw her in the late 90's. Probably because I was wearing an off-shoulder blouse and tossing my hair around. Don't you wish we could relive the relish of imagining ourselves the heroines of such tales. If we were to analyze this fascination with handsome pirates who wanted to kidnap us, we might attribute it to innocence. Love and lust (whatever that was?) were beautiful, exciting . . . . and very mysterious . . . to us at that age. How wonderfully delicious to experience the adventures as we imagined them. During a recent meeting of our journaling group, we each drew a word from the hat and were to write a small piece in a 10 minute drill. My word was "brazen." What could be better? There, forever in my memory, was an experience so familiar I cannot say whether it was Yerby's imagination or mine. Following our class's gifted poets through frosted flora and other woodland encounters; just after the beautifully crafted dialogs from the real writers in the group who drew hard words such as "metaphor" or "litigious," I read: ***Standing at the*** *frigate's bow in gleaming nakedness, the brazen hussy flung back her heavy cape of auburn ringlets and, poised at the edge of her life as Lady Josephine, dove into the sea and began to swim toward the pirate ship.* Now, that's the good stuff. love, jojo

10.2.16   Shoveling Greatness

Burba, I received a phone call from Florida this morning. My friend Annie had left her goldfish in my care, packed up the new pink shirt and left for the Gulf Coast. I missed her first call because I was out shoveling snow. Trapped in the worn and deflated down jacket, I clomped along behind the shovel in the vintage snowmobile boots. Push, lift, push, lift one square of sidewalk at a time toward the edge of the driveway. Wearing a cap requires a fashion choice. Leave it back behind bangs or pull it over them. Before long, the cap usually makes this decision, adding an inch or two downward. Thus I make my way visually impaired, nose dripping, socks slipping into little balls near the toes in the clumsy boots. I knew somewhere people turned their SPFed faces to the sun and walked shoeless.

Tonight I will scavenge up the weekend's leftover olive dip and broken Triscuits to make a little party while I see winter with new eyes via satellite. In Vancouver, where everyone looks happy in the snow, the whiteness becomes an element of Olympic greatness; and as if I were there, standing in the old boots, I'll cheer . . . . Go World. Love, jojo

10.2.24   Hospital Ship

On Monday, our cruise line gave us an upgrade to a top deck suite. On Tuesday, Fox & Friends announced that our ship was having the plague some place in Caribe but who can give up a free suite for a little case of diarrhea? So off we go Friday morning with pills and wipes galore. Love you, Barbara

B, Hope you are enjoying this day at sea . . . sans pills and wipes. Granddaughter Abbygail and I drove to Green Bay yesterday where she boarded a flight to Aruba. We stopped at Old Navy in GB where my little princess picked up a new shirt and a $4.00 sundress for the trip. One more stop for a couple of granola bars, and she was on her way. Her husband, Justin, left shortly after from Houghton to make a presentation in Phoenix on his PhD project for Mich Tech. Molly and 7 other Sigma Kappas board a ship in Puerto Rico this morning for an Eastern Caribe cruise. She has had some good job offers, so this may be her last vacation for a while. Did we miss out on something at this age???? I don't recall tropical islands or cruises in my past. I'm happy that my g.children have these adventures. Life and responsibilities will come at them pretty quickly in the near future.

Jeff and Laurie are driving over today to sit by the fire with me and we can keep each other from wondering if the girls are staying in a group and wearing their sunscreen. Also, the bulldog, who cries when he sees a suitcase in the front hall, needs cheering. So, Barb and Earl, please dance on the deck, sing in the bar, eat the mints on your pillows. Sandy Sister and I will sign on someday. I'm putting away a little every month and should be able to ensure a nice little closet above the bilge pumps. So what . . . everyone says you don't spend any time in your room unless you've hooked up with the ballroom dance instructor.

```
10.8.3
```

```
Oh, how soon we forget: (You and I) Boarded
luxury school bus and arrived at Brevort
Lake. Sat on grass and ate lunches packed by
ourselves. Went for wonderful lake adventures
in leaky row boats. Talked about boys and
getting summer jobs. BofBB
```

10.2.24   Sign Me Up

BBofB, To shorten up this winter, I have signed up for every group that is meeting within a 50 mile radius of Jack's Restaurant: i.e., Family & Community Service Association, Ladies Aid, Altar Guild, Journal Group, Rapid River Readers, Card Club, Quilting Circle, and, as a consequence of all the meeting refreshments . . . TOPS (Take Off Pounds Sensibly). The most recent and enjoyable evenings are in a class on songwriting. Singing and guitar are involved; and I always come away with little lyrics continually beating at my brain. The need to set everything to music is becoming an obsession. "Dishwashing Blues" "Bird Feeder Ballad" "Lo-Fat Pizza Polka" (the latter is a nice combination of where I am in life). The writers' group meets twice monthly, and is a comfortable and inspiring group of 8. I'm, as usual, over my head; but, I feel it is a learning experience, and members challenge and encourage each other. A recent writing exercise somehow evolved from a "cabin" story to Dad's friendship with Jimmy the Indian. Was hard to keep it strictly fictional, but there are enough pieces of fantasy to qualify. See if you can find them. Love from jojo

10.2.25   Jimmy The Indian

My dad and Jimmy the Indian were fishing partners and good friends. No failure to observe political correctness here, the name was said as if all one word. There was no disputing his heritage. He was all 66 inches . . . on a tall day . . . American Indian, his skin the deepest shade of maple. He was lean and strong enough to wrestle bears, but he hadn't. His face should have made the movie screen in a Western film, except he didn't trust horses. At one time, he could have worn the straight black hair longer, but his spikey brushcut was a wise concession to a lower profile in those days. Also, Uncle Cal was a barber, and he traded haircuts for the pleasure of Jimmy's latest views on life. As for the pc name thing, he called my dad Ed, but when they were kidding around, which was most of the time, dad was 'Kimosabe.' Jimmy said that was Chippewa for horse's ass.

Jimmy the Indian a/k/a Jimmy Smith, and wife, Daisy, lived on Bay Mills Point. No one clearly recalls the small house; however, we remember everything about the yard Jimmy had created. He would credit his talent for landscaping as a personal gift to him from the Great Spirit. As children, we could roam through the arbors, over the little bridge and among the small corners of beach rock and wildflowers. Everything has been gone for years, but I still hope to see something left of his handiwork when I drive by the overgrown homesite.

Landscaping being mostly seasonal, winters found my dad and Jimmy doing some old-time trading. Groceries from dad's store were shared with the Smiths when needed. In exchange, painting, repairing and improving our home was a united effort. My parents owned a three story house with two other apartments besides our own; and we were always happy to see Jimmy at the door. In the spring, mother and Daisy would wash and oil each log in our cabin on Bay Mills and, feeling safety in numbers, would banish all nesting mice. We picked wild blueberries, really small wild strawberries and raspberries together, making jam at the cabin over mother's kerosene stove. There were no obligations in this arrangement, only friendship.

Three little girls, gathered around the ladder he worked from, grew up believing native lore according to Jimmy. He claimed to be half Chippewa, half Baptist. He smoked only "vitaminized" cigarettes. We know our dad must have heard years of good stories as together they fished the Bay and into Canada. During his first trip back to a favorite place after Jimmy's death, dad told us about sitting in the boat alone, missing him. A butterfly kept coming back to land on his shoulder each time he brushed it away. Dad said he then remembered Jimmy saying Indians could return to life as a forest creature; and he felt as if Jimmy was still there. He was only surprised that his fierce Chippewa-Baptist friend had chosen to be a butterfly.

Jimmy the Indian died in the early fall on the day of the corn moon. His ancestors celebrated this time of plenty and the season's beauty in their woodlands. Permission given by the tribe allowed my dad to walk on sacred land. Thus, Ed, a/k/a/ Kimosabe, helped carry his friend through the brightest color of the hardwoods to the tall fireweed and sweetest grass of the burial grounds overlooking Lake Superior. I like to think dad and Jimmy are fishing together again. I remember the butterfly story each time I see one. If there are two together, I wonder . . . .

10.3.7   Princess

Abby, Sometimes the heart sends out a message, and the message becomes a thought. That big corner of my heart which is exclusively yours provides me with countless pleasant and/or fun moments. I was following a salt truck out to the highway this grey morning, randomly checking my mental list of "city" errands, when thoughts of you just popped right out of my heart. One of my memories of you returned . . . . in which you are bundled, crying, in your first winter snowsuit on a day like this when you had come for a visit. During those first months of tiny colicky tummy, you were occasionally referred to as "Crabby Abby." However, that day , still a baby, you had no other way to protest all that bundling . . . Only your scrunched up eyes were showing when I put you on my lap. And, lo, as I unzipped, unsnapped and untied you, the crying quieted, the beautiful eyes opened and looked up at me with gratitude. And you smiled at your gramma. A little thought rose up then, and I recognized what a lovely discovery you are! By the time I passed Gladstone this morning, I figured out why I always feel peaceful about you . . . I've known since that day you are beautiful from the inside out, as well as being pretty as a princess. Love, gramma

10.3.10   Mouse In The House

BBofB, Had the first mouse of the season come to visit. Came right out of the closet in the tv room, looked at me, then scooted off. So, I went to Mel's Feed and Garden Store to buy some new traps . . . one of which was the sticky glue type. Of course, I caught the mouse in that. This meant his teeny whiskers and tail and feet were all stuck in the glue and he was looking up at me with sad eyes. Yikes! I took the mouse with attached trap to the garage and spent what seemed like ages (to both of us) trying to get him/her out of the glue, petting the poor trembling creature all the way through the ordeal. I managed to free it, but had to put it out at the tree line with very sticky little body. Last I saw of the mouse, it was trying to scurry off, collecting debris on its fur as it made its way into the woods. Maybe it will survive because it is so cleverly camouflaged. It's the best I could do. Note to Me: Buy more humane traps from Mel.

10.5.8   Pie Sundays and Graduations

BBofB, Happy Mother's Day! I am baking pies in preparation for the annual "Pie Sunday." Yearly, the ladies of the quilting group bake 3 pies each to provide a special coffee hour following church. One pie is cut up to serve, the other two are sold off to raise money for our quilting supplies for the next year. Counting on a full house for Mother's Day services, the event is traditionally held second Sunday in May. The house does smell good . . . like apple macaroon pie, old fashioned apple pie and fresh rhubarb custard. The apples are from Stonington's Wolf River trees, and the rhubarb came from my absent neighbors' yard.

Nearing the end of his life, a member of my family was brought to the VA Hospital in Iron Mountain. My sister, Sandy, called to tell me about walking into his room and seeing the beautiful handmade quilt on his bed. At some time, a corner of the quilt was turned, and she saw the little label Rebecca had sewn there: *Trinity Lutheran Church, Stonington.* It was heartening, my sister told me, to feel the connection to me and to Auntie Carol at that time. I remember helping deliver the quilts that were sewn for the hospital, walking into the rooms and placing a colorful quilt on each bed. Steve Borg was a lifetime Lutheran, active in his church in Marquette. He died comforted, beneath a Lutheran quilt, surrounded by those who loved him and the love of those who had never met him.

The dual graduations went off well. Jeff and I greatly enjoyed the speaker at Abby's ceremony at Michigan Tech. President Emeritus Ray

Smith told wonderfully amusing and inspiring stories about working his way up from the hobo camps in the depression to a job digging foundations (with a shovel!) for the first building at U of Alaska. He shoveled alongside the first president of that university who enrolled Smith as part of his pay, helped him acquire books and his degree. I think there could be a play on this story using parts of Obama's speech heard at Molly's U of Michigan graduation, which Laurie attended. What are the odds of raising two daughters who would distinguish themselves at separate universities, and graduate on the same day. As you know, my heart was heavy for Jeff and Laurie who had to divide the day, but with all the modern texting and telephone photos, we managed to all be together.

On to AmyJo's wedding in June. I have come up with the outfit everyone is asking about. I will wear the dress I wore for our 50th class reunion. I then cut it to an afternoon length for Abby's wedding. I feel comfortable in it. It is suitable. It is paid for. AmyJo will be so beautiful, no one will notice me.

While in Houghton for the graduation, we drove over to Hubbell to a little Finn café for breakfast. Along the lake shore we passed all those interesting ruins from the early mining. Much of the stamp sand is being hauled away, and the sites are being "revegitated" for building. I thought it was mysterious in that area. One wonders what is still under the earth. Some say there is much copper left, and to the south and west in the U.P. there is evidence of gold.

A gold rush near Stonington! Looking forward to your trip up here!!! Love, jojo

10.6.5   Married on a Mountaintop

Two days ago our plane skirted the Blue Ridge Mountains and landed in Roanoke, Virginia. My granddaughter, AmyJo, was waiting to drive me the rest of the way up the mountain where she would be married on June 5th. Amy of the generous heart had lost it to Lance Golden II. Even as a little girl, she seemed to overflow with kindness and genuine caring for every member of her large family of parents, brother Ryan, grandparents and countless aunts, uncles and cousins. She is a devoted and loved friend. In fact, Amy was so grounded in family and friends, we all thought she would never settle far from us, despite her studies to become a teacher. Not that we were surprised that such a beautiful girl would find love . . . only that it would be in Virginia. Driving up the mountain road together, I had to touch her arm as I did when she was a child, affirming the love I feel for her.

AmyJo Beggs and Lance Golden II were married atop Bent Mountain surrounded by family and friends. The day and the setting were lovely. But nothing could outshine the bride. Love you always RoBeDo!! gram

10.8.16   The House Is Okay

Deej,

Just to let you know I have been looking after your property in your absence. All is okay with your house. We cleaned it up really well after the fire. Fortunately, your vehicle had been stolen before the blaze; so, if the State Police find it, it should be in good shape. anniecat had run away before all this. It was a clever escape through a small tunnel she had dug under the litter pan, abetted, I'm sure, by the snarky looking tomcat she was spotted romancing behind the Swallow Inn. The Animal Control People are on the lookout for her, and I will claim her as soon as I see her photo in the shelter ad . . . . hopefully before they put the URGENT writing on it. I wasn't able to save the barrels of deer feed . . . . but you will find a use for all that popped corn at Christmas. love from auntie jojo

August 18th

P.S. Good news and bad news regarding your truck. Good news is it has been located. Bad news is it showed up in the demolition derby at the fairgrounds. The driver ran off to avoid arrest without paying his race entry. You can take care of this by sending a check to the UP Fair

Board. They will need reimbursement for towing charges also . . . plus a beer tab at the grandstand. Your auntie jojo

August 20th

Just a note to suggest you make arrangements for housing before you return. Your friends on the Ensign Twp Volunteer Fire Dept. say it will be several days before the fire scene cools down. It was really disheartening when the original fire re-ignited yesterday. They tried to save your camper, but those pesky sparks made it all the way to the pole barn. And if you will contact the State of Michigan with a credit card number, they will see that the charges owing the Fair Board are paid. The State Police will then cancel the warrant and All Points Bulletin they have issued, and you can re-enter Michigan. I cleared up the Amber Alert matter right away, convincing them the missing annie was actually a cat. Yes, well, anniecat looked so fetching in the shelter photo, she was adopted by a Republican before I could drive to town and claim her. She is on her way to Iowa for the caucuses. Not wanting to disappoint you, I am continuing to watch your house as requested. I have been driving by daily to check the ruins and marvel at the small herds of animals now grazing on the popcorn which is covering your property. Hope you had a wonderful vacation. See you soon. Love auntie jojo

10.9.21   Forest Creature

BBofB, Fall is approaching . . . temps in the 30's overnight. Everyone seems to be invigorated. We Yoopers have been living in the woods so long we take on the habits of forest creatures preparing for winter: cleaning up the nest for the long weeks of hibernation; storing up food (dilly beans and tomato pickle); and traveling all over the countryside to engage in social activity before the roads freeze over. In addition to dragging the flannel sheets off the top shelf in the linen closet and canning the beans and tomatoes this past week, I signed up for the final "fun day" at the golf club with Annie and El, volunteered to sub in the "bunco" club for the winter months, and renewed my ties to the Rapid River Readers and Stonington Ladies Card Club. I quit shaving my legs now that shorts season is over, and am beginning to blend into the aforesaid "forest creature" image. jojo

10.10.14   Woefully Empty

BBofB, Abby has settled into married life on MTU campus where Justin completes work on his PhD. She works as a personal banker for Wells Fargo. Molly is setting up projects for Capital One and a new life for herself in Richmond, Virginia. This leaves Jeff and Laurie to pause at the doors to their daughters' vacant bedrooms. They check with each other hourly for word from their two chicks. I found Jeff and the bulldog slouched in a chair last week wearing the same mournful expression, and Laurie was trying to fill up the afternoon with a nap. There were no muffins or cookies cooling on their kitchen countertop which, like the rest of the house, seemed woefully empty. gramma jojo who misses them, too.

10.11.15   Hunting Season at Menards

Burba, Hunting season is upon us! Elmer's County Market is full of (a) couples shopping together for hunting camp staples, such as cheap hams, Kraft Macaroni and Cheese mixes, Wonder bread and bologna; and (b) freshly whiskered men here early to stock their camps with cartloads of beer, brandy and Bush's beans.

I try to stand in line behind the guys wearing LL Bean boots buying steaks and Cabernet. I have my lists ready for Menard's where, this season, I hope to improve my skills in casual conversation in the electrical and portable deer blind departments. Last year's encounter in motion sensors caught me unprepared, and I missed out on a great opportunity to discuss yard lights with a tall, grey haired stranger. Menard's house brand bridge mix is surprisingly palatable, and I will restock before card club next month. Last year I bought my Christmas cards there, another excuse to scout the plumbing aisles.

Weather is remarkably warm and sunny. I'm sorry I put all the deck furniture away because I find myself sitting on the back steps with my morning coffee or standing on the walkway to watch the sunsets, holding on to these good days as long as possible. Such reveries are interrupted by the aforesaid hunting season preparation when nearby hunters sighting in their rifles fire off occasional blasts which reverberate through the treetops sounding as if they are loading up for large elephants . . . which is what it sounds like to my squirrels and chipmunks also. Thinking they are safe during elephant season, they keep munching on my bird seed without lifting their fat cheeks from the feeders.

My kids are off to Mexico on an adventure and I am taking care of the bulldog. This will be my adventure. I will stay at their house because if he escapes I will know where to find him. He runs away to two locations, only: the nearby ice cream shop and Webster School. His bulldog brain has these two sites programmed as prime territory for tasty handouts.

Tomorrow I'll report on the annual Hunter's Spaghetti Feed prepared by our Ladies Aid. Held each year in downtown Stonington, the 'All You Can Eat' meal is served up for the benefit of our beloved little Lutheran. My post—menopausal self and contemporaries will hover over steaming pots in the throes of our hot flashes while the required hairnets slip down our sweaty brows. All for a good cause, but not, as you suggested, a good situation for making an impression on some interesting single hunter, hungry enough to leave the camp cocktail party. love, Smelt Goddess.

11.2.15   First Day of Summer

BBof B: On Sunday I drove to church through the Yooper monsoon season. Raining, raining, raining . . . . and then the wind came up and blew us, at gusts up to 40 mph, into Monday morning. As the winds died, and the salt trucks tried to restore some sort of surface to the roads, we all realized the temperature was above freezing for the first time since the opening day of deer season. It is now Tuesday, and with temperatures still rising towards a predicted high of 56° on Thursday (THIS week, not next June, dear), we are taking the felt liners from the boots, trying on the white slacks and washing out the hummingbird feeders. We don't care what the Mayans say . . . this is summer. If the next Alberta clipper reaches us on Friday, dropping the temperatures back below zero, we will call it a "cold spell" and keep shoveling a path to the garden shed where the tiki torches are stored.

I am currently busy learning a new word processing program for the laptop. The installed program appears to be funded by companies which want to sell you another program through advertising. These ads pop up in the margins of my email and blink in and out of the verses I'm typing for the Ladies Aid devotions. Fortunately, the merchants of anti-wrinkle products and cures for sexual dysfunction have not yet acquired my new address. However, I proofread all my handouts verrrry carefully.

How are things for you this week? Was hoping to hear your nephrologist was a romantic and gave you a helpful set of dialysis hardware for Valentine's Day. But, it sounds as if he still plans this for some date later. Meanwhile, hope the blood and procrit is allowing you to keep up with the ironing and stay awake for all the revolutions on the nightly news. I'm out of funny things to say . . . call me if you need me. Love you, jo

11.2.7 Yooper Crime

Last month, a man wearing camouflage pants, dark colored jacket and baseball cap got out of a car parked on a side street in downtown Rapid River, Michigan. He carried a concealed weapon. Up to this point, his description fit a large number of the male population in the Upper Peninsula. However, pulling a ski mask over his face, he walked down the street and entered a credit union where he threatened tellers with a pistol. After acquiring an "undisclosed" amount of cash, he left the scene on foot.

In minutes, law enforcement personnel were on the roads to Rapid River. Officers from the Michigan State Police posts in Gladstone and Manistique were first to reach the area, and were joined in the investigation by the 8th District Homeland Security Team from Marquette, the Delta County Sheriff's Department, the Menominee County K-9 Unit, Gladstone and Escanaba Public Safety Departments and the Upper Peninsula Substance Enforcement Team detectives, causing one highly perceptive reporter to write: "With that many people after you, you don't' stand a chance." He was right. Within a short time a young man.was apprehended. He was barely 21 years of age. The money he had used to rent an apartment for himself was traced back to the credit union. His 19 year old friend will go to prison also. He provided the transportation that afternoon, and had purchased a small air pistol used in the robbery.

This story of the Rapid River Robbery began in a more lighthearted vein. It was to be an undocumented account of Yooper crime and punishment, told as some events are told in rural areas, from house to house or over morning coffee at the Donut Connection. Such as:

On Wednesday, January 19th, the first report of misfortune in the area reached Stonington with Ken and Carol Mosher. They were driving home from Tractor Supply in Escanaba when Michigan State Police cars passed them, fully lit (the cars, not the Moshers), at a high rate of speed. Ken guessed there was a bad road accident on some strip of black ice laid by recent weather. Clara Benesch was also on her way home that afternoon when police vehicles "went flying past her." She, too, thought there had been some tragedy on the highway.

According to earliest local stories, the robber left the credit union and walked across the street to the Swallow Inn. There he joined a friend at the bar as police, government agents, bomb sniffing dogs, et al., began Crime Scene Investigation 60 yards away. Since their bank robbing attire strictly conformed to the Swallow Inn dress code, the two men did not arouse suspicion; and, eventually they departed the bar and drove away from Rapid River.

Employees of the family-owned Pantry Truck Stop (Jerky! Fudge!! Smoked Fish!!) worried about the possible loss of business in a high crime area. Residents cast fearful looks south toward Detroit and wondered how soon their community would be a police drama on late night TV. The new proprietors of the Bait Shop and All-Types Engine Repair had their own concerns. How long would it be, they agonized, before Rapid River's unchallenged title to Walleye Capital of the World would be revoked. Fishing tournaments were scheduled, and the Lions Club was already painting the new "Welcome Fishermen" signs. That night, with criminals on the loose, all Wednesday choir practices were cancelled. Children were excused from Jan Lundin's catechism class. Residents who heretofore left their doors unlocked while they went on winter vacation, bolted up their homes.

Within a week the criminals were apprehended. There was quiet disappointment at the post office where Sally had cleared a place for its first FBI "Two Most Wanted" poster.

The accounts of their arrest were varied, but my personal favorite is the rice pudding story which described a daring capture of the two felons in Escanaba's Swedish Pantry while they enjoyed Phyllis's famed dessert. Later, some would say this narrative was manufactured by Phyllis for business reasons, a theory that has now cast doubt upon the Swallow Inn story.

Late in the investigation, a plausible part of the time frame was credited to customers of Jack's Restaurant on the corner of US2 and Rapid River's "Miracle Half Mile." They now recall a man wearing a ski mask was observed walking by the streetside windows. Since the windows were somewhat steamy from the fryers and their attention was drawn to the luncheon special before them, his covered face didn't register on the diners. The fact that a man bent on armed robbery would walk, masked, down main street to the crime scene calls for a better word than plausible.

Following the robbery, a yellow crime scene tape was placed across the entrance to the credit union, causing a steady stream of traffic driving by to see it. As recorded, this was January in the Upper Peninsula. We *all* drove into Rapid River to see the tape. Nancy Diehl and her card club had a group picture taken in front of it. And there were reports of FBI sightings. The Lorenson sisters, Hawaiina and

Rose, were sure they saw an FBI car with two men in it . . . . agents, certainly.

The Rapid River Robber was actually apprehended quietly in his parents' home a short time after he took the money he used to rent an apartment. He admitted to the robbery and returned a good portion of the cash taken. He and his accomplice were taken to a jail in Marquette and will go from there to prison. The young man who held up the credit union faces a probable sentence of 25 years. When I asked questions for this story, I could hear an underlying sadness for them. I heard "personable" and "not a trouble-maker" frequently. However, they took money that didn't belong to them. To accomplish this, they bought a weapon and used it to terrorize three women, one of whom is still distressed by the experience. Sometimes a story can begin as fun, but when the events have lead to suffering and wasted lives, you cannot end it on a happy note.

11.7.10   Spangles and Big C-Burgers

Moll, I do not like these first days after everyone leaves . . . . Seems as if one day we are all bar-b-quing, swimming, jetskiing, bonfiring, and the next thing you know everyone is gone, leaving the house empty (except for the sad pile of damp towels and a refrigerator full of sloppy Jo's). I am forced to rally today and prepare to hostess the Ladies Aid tonight. All those good Swedish Lutheran housekeepers are coming to my sad little digs where a leftover soda can could roll out from under the sofa at any time. I have prepared a fresh lemon dessert, putting me out of the competition for the recipe containing the most chocolate and nuts everyone seems to prefer. Besides, I have lost 3 pounds since I left my TOPS group, which qualifies me to talk about weight loss at the class reunion this weekend in the Soo. My 60th. YIKES!! Am I supposed to be old, Molly?? To dispel this image, I will attend in a tiered skirt with spangles sewn on the bottom tier. My friend Barb and I found this in a consignment shop in Beaufort, SC. At 16 bucks for the skirt, I could afford a new white scoop neck tee which shouldn't go to war with all those spangles, the cost of which includes a donation for homeless animals. (I am NOT kidding). I'll not sit next to Helen who will be there dressed in Boca Grande Simple Chic. After the reunion party and my weight loss are history, I'll head for the Sugar Island ferry dock and a Clyde's "Big C-Burger." You were missed over the 4th little girl, but we have good times ahead when you get home again. You have a new and exciting life where you are . . . and we are always here waiting for you. love, gramma

P.S. Thank you for the stirring Picasso. It is an amazing puzzle I am enjoying each time I see it on the fridge. Now that Picasso outfit would cause a stir at my reunion!!

11.10.2   Endangered Species

BBofB, My oil delivery man, who appreciates me supporting his lavish lifestyle as I deplete the oil reserves, has passed on this happy report: the big perch have returned off Garden and are plentiful. This was told with such enthusiasm, I take it as a real event. I then recalled one year when we baited the hooks in shifts because they were biting so fast just off downtown Garden., We were with another couple . . . Jeff and Laurie???? Anyway, I remember it was the women who did most of the baiting shifts because we were using worms and I was being a good sport. Also, I hear they are taking wolves off the endangered species list. I am hoping the wolves will be taking me off their grocery list as a show of good faith in the truce. This would not affect my rating with the marauding bear(s) who are terrorizing the Stonington peninsula. Jeff has seen the evidence in my back yard with his own eyes. If I am carried off while eating a Snickers bar as I walk to the mailbox, my last words will be addressed to him: "I told you so!" I try to wear colorful and recognizable clothing while outdoors in case he needs further proof of my old story about the Bay Mills Bear Hunt. I have my future oriental lily garden in the ground and covered with pepper, deer spray, bounce sheets and guarded by my garden gnome. jojo

11.11.27   Three Thanksgivings

Burba: I remember a recent movie titled "Four Christmases." Today's note is captioned "Three Thanksgivings." Laurie and Jeff set the table on Thanksgiving Day for Molly, home from Richmond, Justin and Abby, on loan from Michigan Tech, Cousin DJ and me representing the Stonington clan. When the time came to recite our blessings, Jeff declared he was grateful for enough wages to pay for such a generous meal. Everyone was moved. I then told the family about seeing a young man in Elmer's Market holding a can of soup as he stood looking into the case of bacon, hot dogs, etc. He was there for the time it took me to cover two aisles, and I sensed he was pricing the items and struggling to make a choice. I wished I could have helped him. Jeff had to cover the moment with his usual surface cynicism, trying to lighten our thoughts by claiming the poor fellow was sent by his wife to pick up a special brand of hot dogs and had forgotten what she ordered. He stood there worried like most men on the brink of a failed mission, Jeff claimed. But, even this typical Jeff whimsy couldn't cover the highlight of his original and true feelings about a bountiful Thanksgiving surrounded by his family. The next day I had only to travel down 513 to spend Thanksgiving II with Tom, Pam and Kellee who had arrived to celebrate the holiday in their cabin. It was a cozy celebration by the wood fire with just the four of us. Tom and Pam always have Copper Country history and good stories of natives to share, including background on the "Sweater Letter" book I had just finished. Kellee filled me in on the "walk-in" she and her friends plan at the school. It is good for grammas to hear about such healthy fun. Today is the third day of celebration, and the sloppy jo, baked beans, macaroni and cheese are underway. We will all gather under one roof for this meal, and I, like Jeff, will be thankful for the bounty. And the joy of being surrounded by family. jojo

12.2.1   Waiting Princess

Dearest Princess Abby, There you are confined to the tower waiting
for your little prince (or princess) to arrive. Sorta a new slant on an
old tale, isn't it. This is good that you are home and can try to be more
comfortable. Here are some "don'ts" for you. 1. Do not watch reruns
of the primary debates on news channels. The baby may pick up bad
vibes and end up a career protester carrying little signs everywhere.
2. Do not have ice cream in the freezer. It has an evil power over me
which you may have inherited. 3. Do not watch from the windows at
the outside world. Neighbors' children will think you are the creepy
old lady who won't buy Girl Scout cookies. 4. Do not while away
time looking at "Hairdo" or "Elle" magazines. Chances are when you
and your hormones are friends again you will not like the paprika hair
color you are planning on; and it will be a while before you wear the
lime green cargo shorts you are thinking of ordering. Instead, put those
little feet (you remember, they are attached to that area of your body
you haven't seen for a while) up and open your book to a wonderful
adventure somewhere. But remember to shuffle around to small
chores intermittently which don't require standing too long. Keep the
circulation moving, then back to rest. Sometime in the not too distant
future, you will think of these hours when you were supposed to
lounge around as the good old days. Meanwhile, call me anytime, text
me, drop me an email. I'm here thinking of you and counting the days
with you. hugs and love from gramma (soon to be "gg")

12.8.20   Squirrel Olympics

BBofB: This is the week I turn over the remains of my potted plants,
herb garden and perennials to the squirrels and chipmunks. It is the
end of another summer of defeat in the war of wits. The herbs were
the first to go, their tasty roots a first course at the annual banquet
held by the Twin Springs Chipmunk Legion. Not to be outdone in
healthful choices, the squirrels nibbled through a daily salad from
my pots of hybrid daisies, neatly grazing on each pot so that the
devastation was uniform. You have to respect that about squirrels.

So here they are scampering from one side of the yard to the other through a ground cover of acorns from my too generous oak trees. Aren't they supposed to be eating acorns . . . or at least gathering them? It's because of Facebook and texting . . . too much information available about herbs, perennials and such. The major factor, however, in my recent concession is the Battle of the BIRDfeeder. A birthday gift from Jeff, beautifully designed as a lighthouse and built by him, the feeder is 3 feet tall and nearly as wide. Filled with seeds, it sits atop a 7' length of drainpipe at what should be a safe distance from trees and branches. A bird has yet to touch down on the BIRDfeeder. Under new management, it is now the local squirrel Golden Arches and site of their 2012 Olympics. Located just outside the window in my dining area, diners have an opportunity to watch squirrels flying from the trees to "stick" landings on the feeder. It has been moved several times to conform to our calculations of how far a squirrel can leap from the nearest branches. There is also an interesting display of metal stove pipe up and down trees surrounding the feeder which lends a new level to scoring an event, although it detracts somewhat from the mood of a woodland setting. If you are fortunate enough to be here when the BIRDfeeder runs out of BIRDseed, and the squirrels are bored with my plantings, you will be treated to a matinee performance of their scratching on the windows or climbing up and down the screens for attention. jojo

12.10.9   Losing Streak

JoJo: Why is YOUR football team so bad this year? Love from a bunch of new Vikings Fans

Dear Mr. and Mrs. Disgruntled:

Welcome to the Vikings Fan Club,

Due to the recent surge in membership in our Green Bay district, official Viking jerseys and "Packers Suck" bumper stickers are in short supply. However, we are forwarding our brochure on redecorating with purple. We are also sending you two gift certificates for a free lutefisk lunch during halftime at our cozy sheltered stadium. Remember, it's 80% off all Brett Favre memorabilia at the nearby Mall of America!! Go Vikings . . . .

Dear Viking Fan Club: We found the booklet on "Decorating in Purple" very helpful. Because we spent the morning laughing at your letter, we were unable to finish knitting the toilet seat cover that you recommended. Darn! That great Viking carpeting is on back order. The 80% sale of Brett Favre stuff seems to explain why Earl cannot sell his "Brett, you are My Hero" sweatshirt on ebay. I hope everyone in your neighborhood is looking forward to the Packer game with the Texans. Since they have only won five out of five it should be a real fun shootout for the Seniors over at the home. Sending you my special recipe for purple cheese dip by snail mail.

Love from the Land of the Carolina Cardinals.

Annie, El and I had fun with your Vikings membership letter over coffee. El is still on pain pills after knee surgery the other day so we left the booze in the cupboard and were more or less clear-headed at the time. This allowed us to realize we know where we had seen all the Vikings carpet!! At first we thought it had been the Escanaba Elks Club because the color matches all their secret fraternal stuff, but then recalled the new footing behind the salad bar at the C'mon Inn. The dim lighting there may leave this conclusion still open for debate . . . and the areas of droppings from Emmie's famous double dressing potato salad have distorted the pattern on the floor. However, the area covered would be large enough to qualify for consideration. Comprising nearly two blocks of prime Rapid River downtown real estate, the salad bar is without equal in the quest for new ways to use mayonnaise and grated Velveeta. Mountains of jello quiver with every imaginable ingredient, including . . . as rumored . . . leftovers from last Friday's fish fry. I'm sorry that you missed out on Viking carpeting, but wait until the playoffs . . . you may have to change your decor to Black if the Saints can keep Brees healthy. love from jojo

```
Hi Jojo, The Old South Discount Carpet and Flea
Market was able to put a roll of purple carpet
on hold. They say a "Clay" color is very big
in Wisconsin right now. In other news, Earl
discovered that if he turned his "Brett You are
My Hero" sweatshirt inside out it says, "I am
still with you Aaron." So he removed it from
ebay. BofBb
```

Burba, Our Detroit Tigers are putting the hurt to the Yankees and have come away with the first two games (at Yankee Stadium!!) on the way to a pennant. Laurie and I stayed with them into overtime and through 12 innings Saturday nite, falling into our beds at 1:14 a.m. We were still barely awake when Sunday's Game 2 began at 4 p.m. Because the Packers met the Texans at 8 that evening . . . well, I missed a couple of Nelson's TD's while dozing off occasionally then waking to try and focus on who was at bat. If I had known being a sports fan was so grueling, I would have trained harder. The Clay Matthews jersey from Jeff, Laurie and their clan is my game day attire. This was its first duty as a nightshirt. Am almost disappointed that the Pack did so well without me. I was awake, however, when Rogers was asked, post-game, how he had handled recent concerns about his performance. "How did you reply to these questions?" Answering that, Rogers put his finger to his lips and whispered "Shhhhhhhh." Lovely, just lovely Aaron. You are Our Hero, too. Love jojo

12.10.29   Hurricane Sandy

Barb: Right now the wind is gusting over 50 mph on our little Squaw Point. Coming straight out of the north, the waves are running nearly sideways, and the whitecaps in front of my place look like something out of last nite's CNN News. I made my way to the garage earlier, hanging on to the little rail on the bridge . . . . All I needed was a microphone and a red rain jacket to be mistaken for a newscaster.

The duck blind is still standing and some sorry geese are clustered around it, mistaking it, in their little goose brains, for a sanctuary. The seagull flights that haven't been canceled are hanging into the wind, motionless against the gale, but still aloft. I was to be in Escanaba this afternoon, but am weighing the cost of gas driving my mighty Honda into the headwind toward Rapid River and avoiding fallen trees on the road. Perhaps I'll just stay to home, open up my new Ian Rankin novel and/or watch the newscasters get blown around on deserted streets. I have friends in Breezy Point, retired firemen and wives, who act like neighbors wherever they are. Always find them in their own group, and they do call themselves "the Breezies" as reported. Those homes at Breezy Point were earned by hard and dangerous work . . . it is beyond heartbreaking and ironic that they should be lost in a fire. Jo

10.31.12　Nearly November

BBofB, I am staying at home this winter. Jeff installed a beautiful gas boiler. This will greatly improve the comfort of my home, and improve my heating budget. However, this season I filled the propane tank and prepurchased nearly a season's supply of fuel, which put a nick in the travel fund. Actually, the cost of airfare to and from the U.P. is a growing consideration. With the airline cutbacks, our smaller airports are closing or offering severely limited schedules. More desperate or affluent customers are still handing over their cash to surly ticket agents while TSA rummages through their carefully folded undies and miniscule allotment of health and beauty aids. It makes one want to simply get behind the wheel of their pickup and drive to somewhere just below the Mackinac Bridge, which is as far as the price of gas will allow. So, I am readying for winter here on Stonington. The outdoor chairs and picnic tables are stacked in the garden shed. All plants spared by the deer and rabbits are covered and the supply of bird feed is stored in cans by the garage door. The leaves drift down now in a constant, light shower, and we have reached that time when all yard work ceases. The groundcover of acorns and leaves will spend the winter. jojo

Christmas 2012 . . . ADVENT

My second hand artificial tree is still sulking in the crawl space although the boxes of decorations are stacked in the center of the living room. I am debating a trip to the tree plantation for a real tree which I will somehow stuff into the trunk of my Honda and cautiously make my way back to Stonington. I will then sneak this lovely, living and fragrant tree into the house while my friends and neighbors who think live trees belong in the outdoors are not looking or are in Menard's replacing lights for their fake balsams with dim LED's. As my daydreams progress, I see my children and grandchildren being greeted in my Christmas house by a glowing evergreen, fresh from the woods, minus perhaps, a branch or two sacrificed on its trip down US-2 Soon I will take every last scrap out of the Christmas Boxes again and distribute everything around the house. All is will be ready for the children and grands. The guest bedroom looks as if crazed elves have been gathering there. Some of my friends tell me how they "don't bother" with trees and decorations anymore. WHAT?? Someday they may wish they could go back and once again look into the stored treasures of remembered Christmases. The "blob/apple" Jeff made will be on the tree, together with Laurie's cross-stitched decorations and the big paper ornament with MOLLY printed in her little hand. I cannot hang it on the branch without seeing her working away on it. Molly was born after the embroidered ornaments were made, and when she was old enough to notice there was not one with her name on it, she gave us no peace and good will at Christmas until we supplied her with the materials to create her own. JJ

BBofB: As Peter Sellers would ask . . . . how is the "Bimp" on your head? I've nearly fallen off a chair at some gatherings where Tequila was served (in my younger days), and barstools were hazardous. I fell off the deck once during an ice storm. I remember falling off my crutches and into a plant stand while recovering from foot surgery. However, I've yet to fall out of bed . . . when dreaming. So, as usual, you are one up on me. Perhaps you will have to forego eating salami or stuffed olives after a certain hour. People tell me this when I come up with what I think is a good idea. Your, jojo

Jojo, The bimp on my head has worked itself into a black eye which I am able to cover with some makeup that I bought in 1993 (expiration date 2000). I think you are very brave and strong to go for a live tree. We have an eight foot dead one decorated to the nines on the front port. Also four small dead ones around the house and plastic on the fireplace mantle and down the middle of the table with Magnolia blossoms. I declared that this was not the climate for live stuff. I bought Christmasy pine cone tree smell at KMart. How we do suffer in the south having to buy smell. Christmas Church starts at 4:30 Christmas Eve. We will need to be there at 4:00 to get in the family service. Maybe some one will come in and spray while we are gone so that I can keep up with your family gathering about your YuleTide present to them. Congrats on having the energy to do all that you do! I am sure it is much appreciated. Have a wonderful time decorating and celebrating. love, BoBb

Jojo, I hope this letter does not find you hanging out at Menards again in the rusty screw department. Well, I went to clean the oven after endless baking of food for the holidays and, of course, the self cleaning was broken. Oh, clean it with Easy Off says Earl. If I got down on my knees to do that, I would be there until New Years when the cleaning girl would move me so she could do the floors. I go down but not up. The children will arrive to a dirty oven. Yesterday, I made Pecan Pie bites from a recipe book that you gave me. Boy, are they good. No one would want a whole piece of pecan pie but they will eat up all the bites. I have mashed potatoes in the freezer, Chicken Tetrazzinni, chili for Christmas eve. Have to make the Oyster dressing just before I bake it on the 25th and Earl starts to cook five pds. of tenderloin in the dirty oven I imagine your family is also planning something in the back of their minds for this birthday thing. Let's run away and go climb a mountain or something. Love, BofBB

Dearest Burba,

We still have parallel lives . . . My oven did self-clean itself; however, either the fumes from the months of boiled over pies and spattering roasts triggered my classic bronchial thing or . . . leaving the windows and front door open for a couple of hours in 25 degree weather brought on an old-fashioned croup. I missed the lighting of the second advent candle at church and stayed home with my misery to finish decorating my lovely real tree, finishing the job finally at 7:45 p.m. in time for my next dose of Mucinex and the kickoff for the Packers-Lions. As I turned my back to the tree, it fell over, scattering the carefully placed ornaments all over the living room, some in small pieces, as the water poured out of the stand, soaking into the carpet. It was like one of those situations where the adrenaline kicks in and you can lift a Coupe de Ville off your grandchild. I picked up the bad, bad real tree, what was left of all the beautifully hidden strings of lights and remains of the ornaments and half tossed it all into a dry corner like some damn olympic javelin champ. I mixed Clan MacGregor with the Mucinex and fell asleep before halftime of a really good game I wish I had seen. This afternoon my nephew will stop by and help me hold the outcast tree in an upright position while I tie it to the wall with brass coffee cup hooks laced with leftover speaker cable. I, too, made the pecan bites . . . heavenly little treats. Is one of my "go to" recipes. And I am also facing a celebration of sorts in July . . . I think the climb up the mountain sounds like a great excuse to be away. Let's do it. Shall we wear drindles and sing "Climb Every Mountain" in a meadow at the top?? I'm all for it. love you, jojo p.s. As soon as I quit coughing, Menards will let me back into the food section where I plan to shop for bargain size bags of holiday nibbles to amaze the family and distract them from the disheveled final real tree . . . jj

```
Dear  Jo,  We  were  very  sorry  to  hear  about  the
tree  disaster  while  you  should  have  been  in  bed
with  your  croup.  Your  Kids  are  so  lucky  not  to
have  a  Mother  running  around  with  a  can  of  Pine
smell  spray.  BofBB
```

I'm having second thoughts about the advisability of you and me trying to climb a mountain . . . my fear of heights and your disdain for the suggested drindles make this a poor plan. Let's come up with something, however. love from jojo

12.25.12   Christmas 2012

Christmas Eve and I started for Escanaba to attend services with Jeff and family, and soon realized that in the darkness the road was barely visible. Oh no, I'm going blind on Christmas. As if this time was worse than any other to discover you are becoming sightless. I would have to break it to the bulldog that he would be going to leader dog school. After a cautious drive into a stream of vehicles with bright, multi level headlights, I reached the church parking lot and discovered one headlight was out and the other dim with several layers of road salt. A Christmas miracle . . . I was blind and now I see.

This morning I found a beautiful pashima from Istanbul in my package from Scott. I wear it over my flannel p.j.s cooking the chicken gizzards for Jeff's treat. I probably won't make artha Stewart's Christmas edition, but I have a new title . . . gizzards goddess.

Now, on to my 80th year . . . .

13.1.1   Vacuuming Up Christmas

Burba, It is good to hear your lovely park has been restored. I, too, have been on the beach these past days. Weather in the 40's, so have been able to sit on an old log near the duck blind. I can watch our eagles from there as they enjoy easy hunting over the miles of ice. Also, just for the heck of it I took a few practice balls out the other afternoon, and managed some January Yooper golf at the edge of the woods. My Christmas tree is once again in the outdoors, tied to a maple alongside the house to provide a retreat for the birds near the feeders. I will miss the good balsam smell in the house and the cozy lights in the evenings. Yes, I had colored lights . . . . and many, many tattered little ornaments. Some day next summer I'll be vacuuming in that corner with the pointy attachment and find a few leftover needles which I will put in my hand, lift to my face and, as Molly once said, "smell a memory." jojo

13.1.2   Walk on Water

Picture the county road (513) on Christmas Eve from the Stonington Community Park to our little church. For that three miles, each side of the road, our church puts out luminaries which are lit shortly before the evening service. Some Stonington youngsters grew up believing Santa could see this lit pathway, and they have had less spiritual appreciation for its purpose. How could Santa overlook Stonington with the road shining to guide him? Who knows . . . more luminaries, larger candles . . . Perhaps next year you may be able to Google in and see God's work in His country.

Today the bay is frozen shore to shore. The ice fishermen have been hanging back along the shorelines because of the warm weather. It rained the other morning, and there was a film of water over the frozen bay. Watching my neighbor guys slip-sliding around their shacks as they tried to walk was entertaining. The warmer air on the ice caused a mist to hang just over the surface most of the day, making the ice-walkers appear as if they were suspended. This brings love from God's Country . . . where we have learned to walk on water. jojo

13.1.24   Cave Dweller

Greetings from the frozen half of the planet . . .

My little cottage is very energy efficient. Even so, at minus 15 degrees the glass on the (double thermopane) windows is frigid. I have the beach towels (mementos of happier days!) tacked up over the windows on the lake side of the house. This lends a cavelike atmosphere to half of my world, a setting enhanced by the small stack of firewood in the laundry and living rooms which guarantees a supplemental heat source if we lose power. All the schools and social activities are cancelled. The bay, now frozen solid enough to support a highway from Stonington to Gladstone, is uninhabited. Not even the eagles and coyotes have ventured out there for two days. Only the chickadees move around outdoors. Such a tiny creature to be able to withstand this prolonged cold. Last night a water main burst just south of Marquette near the prison entrance. The highway flooded, and froze into a large rink. Road salt at the extreme temp during the night does not help. Remember crossing the Mackinac Bridge when it was far below zero and the sand-salt only polished the ice on the roadbed? Those were exciting times.

Because my social life is at a standstill, I am cleaning uncharted areas of my cave such as the guest room closet (also known as the Final Resting Place of unnecessary but still treasured items) and stirring pots of stews and soups which have lightened the load of little tidbits in my freezer. This makes room for the aforesaid stews and soups . . . and a new generation of tidbits. The temperatures will start to come up today, and by the first of next week we will see 20 degrees ABOVE . . . and it will be February. I will take down the towels. Looking ahead,

I feel almost tropical. I may put pineapple in my salad for the church potluck on Sunday!!! jojo

13.2.7   Cruising

Practically on my way, I can smell the sun oil already. Suddenly, I have a thirst for mojitos and a craving for conch chowder. Am sure I'm overweight . . . suitcase, that is . . . (well, probably the rest of me, too), but will pay the overage so I can include my size L capri pants. I could use some help picking out items from the pile of clothes I have thrown on the floor by the closet. The 50 lb. limit narrows it down considerably, and the size of my clothes cuts the wardrobe to a few important pieces. I've already eliminated underwear. I have a new swim suit; and if the old guys don't faint from the sight, I may have a shipboard romance at the dominoes tournament.

Oh, Barb: Will sit on my suitcase in another attempt to close it. I have to include some frozen pasties at the last minute which the FTL kids requested. Thought I would just throw them in my cargo size purse, but the sniffer dogs might delay me in Detroit. I am in the cheap seat section which is the last row on the plane and a whole country will get off before I do. By the time I get to baggage claim the pasties may be thawed enough to attract the dogs, TSA and Rachel Ray. I wish they would learn how to make pasties in Florida. Perhaps we should open up a shop. Do they have rutabagas there?

P.S. We will set sail next week. I haven't achieved the body I pictured as mine, stretched out on a lounge, toasting in the Caribbean sun as mature gentlemen who were able to make it above decks with their walkers gaze at me admiringly. However, I will pick a spot near the passengers who have been enjoying the all you can eat ice cream, and hope my old body improves by comparison. Weather is still lovely, warm, unreal here. Good thing I won't have to buy the new snow shovel I needed this year. I spent the money on "Savage Tan" oil. Bon Voyage to my Beautiful, Fun Daughter Kimberly Sue Peanut and me. Love, Bahama Mama

13.3.25   Spring

The five squirrels who have adopted me for the winter have shown yet another level of determination. Sheet metal cannot discourage them from leaping onto the feeder. Happy as they are to outwit us, they mostly appear content with grazing on the seeds the birds scatter to the ground. The recent storms have buried birdseed deep into the snowbanks around the bird feeder. Looking out the window, I can see just the heads of squirrels popping out of the snow, disappearing and reappearing. Reminds me of the prairie dogs in Nat Geo. Little sprays of snow shoot upwards occasionally, announcing serious tunneling below. Soon a frosted squirrel face appears, and I imagine it is smiling.

A few days since I began the above story, I'm writing this from within a snowglobe, surrounded by swirling whiteness. I wakened this morning to one of those scenes portrayed on the "December" page of calendars. Trees were bent with fresh snow in a landscape of forms heavily capped and unrecognizable under the night's generous reminder that it is still two days until spring . . . For those who are putting on their sunscreen or trimming the hedges this morning, it would seem an "enchanted" world. If there is no snow shovel by their front door, they could fail to understand that enchantment can wear thin even as it weighs on your roof. A short time ago, the NE wind came up to create a little late season chaos, sending weather advisories streaming across the television screen under a recipe for spring lamb and fresh fruit salad. I am well and patient.

I celebrated St. Patrick's Day at my favorite Italian restaurant with my Swede friends from Stonington. Moving on, my house is decorated with all the favorite old Easter treasures fashioned by children and grandchildren since 1956. They laugh about this, but they go from room to room looking for certain memories. All the children will be here for a visit this summer . . . thinking they should do "something" for my 80th. I protest . . . travel is so expensive, yadayadayada. But it will be wonderful to be with them. The grandchildren are coming at different times during the summer, as their jobs allow. One big marshmallow roast and beer fest. jojo

13.3.31   Easter Sunday

I drove into Escanaba to attend the Easter service with Jeff and Laurie, Abby, Justin and Henrik. The old Presbyterian Church in Escanaba was so familiar, and I couldn't help but let my thoughts turn backward to my children in that setting years ago. Tom, Jeff and Scott in little navy blazers (sizes 2, 4, 6) and Kim toddling around in a budget busting ruffled dress, holding on to her little purse like the Queen of England . . . each of them spotted with random pieces of grass from their baskets and their fingers still sticky with the sweetness of jelly beans and Sayklly chocolate. Many egg salad sandwiches would be served in the next week, justifying the cartons of eggs boiled up to satisfy each child's quota of colors for dyeing, There had to be four packages of Paas dye to ensure a full set of cutouts and transfers for each of the children. One year we experimented with "blowing out" the eggs to produce "beautifully artistic shells which could be kept from year to year like small treasures." Mommy almost had to go to the hospital from puffing a whole future chicken out of a little hole in each big egg; and the fragile shells didn't make it to Easter morning. More than once on Easter afternoons we held a Supplemental Easter Egg Hunt because the count was off that morning. This event was originated by Grampa Ed who thought radiators and inside Gramma the Great's bridge lamp were clever places to hide eggs. Then I looked over at Jeffrey Edward, the size 4 child, who was looking over at his child and smiling. He must have been remembering those Easters Past also. And as we stood to sing "Jesus Christ is Risen Today," we felt joyful knowing this day assures us we will be together, all of us, in Easter Beyond.

13.3.31   Just Eat the Carrot

Happy Easter Dear Henrik . . . You will find a basket from the bunny. Be sure to take the wrappings off the treats before you eat them. DO NOT BE FOOLED by the green crunchy stuff in the bottom of the basket. That is not part of the treat . . . just there to make the basket look like the bunny was really generous. So don't eat that either. Save any purple jelly beans for gg . . . and if you find some little brown ones around your basket . . . definitely don't eat those. You will sort this all out better when you have a few Easters behind you. For now, what is really best for you is the nice carrot you are supposed to leave for the bunny. Eat that. Love to you, Daddy and Princess Mama from gg

On 13.4.3 Mr. Muggins and I showed up at the Delta County International Airport to greet Jeff and Laurie. I know in his doggie dreams he had seen himself welcomed past security as a bomb-sniffing bulldog; however, gramma insisted on waiting away from the terminal; thereby sparing him the embarrassment of not being recognized as brave and useful. So there we are waiting atop a snowbank by the fence when all the intelligence and loyalty of his breed kicks in. The plane appears minutes after he knew it was dropping through the thinning clouds to the South. Gramma had been saying for days: "They'll be home soon . . ." It was Soon!! . . . and he was heading for the terminal. Somewhere behind him he could hear: YOU COME HERE! MUGGINS . . . TREAT . . . TREAT . . . APPLE . . . CARROT . . . . CHEESE . . . .

13.4.12   Bootless

Late in the afternoon yesterday an ill wind from the west began to blow away our hopes for spring. By this morning most of the U.P. awoke in 6" of fresh snow. The Channel 6 meteorologist is beginning to look dispirited as he forecasts more of the same through the weekend. Schools have used up their legal "snow days", and today's cancellations dip further into the summer vacations teachers and students have dreamed of in weather like this. Uncle Ken thought he could take the plow off the front of the truck last week, like a lot of Yooper guys, making for a smoother ride and freeing up parking space at WalMart. Not yet. And if you put your big boots away, this morning you will be digging around for them again unless you had a sort of ritualistic purging of all things winter during last week's spring weather, and they are history, together with the weary jacket that has faded and frayed. But, looking ahead, the temperatures will soar to 40 degrees next week . . . and the strong wind last night has blown the ice out of the Bay from Capt's Lane to the South. Am sitting here, not worrying about boots, waiting out the weather . . .

13.4.14   Golf

And out of the shadow of Tiger Woods, shambling across the perfect green of Augusta, the player they had nicknamed "the duck" is making the groomed darlings of the golf world actually sweat up their designer shirts. Angel Cabrera is so powerful and so dedicated to each contact with the ball, he has been my hero for years. Imagine me glued to the broadcast of the Masters as Cabrera made duck soup of the 3rd round yesterday; and with his son, who caddies for him, strode off the course in first place. If he wins the green jacket, he will enjoy fresh celebrity in the U.S. for a time; but back home in Argentina, where he personally funds distribution of food to children, he is always admired and loved.

Inspired by the past weekend's televised scenes of long, deer-free fairways and velvet greens where the golf balls always seem to land less than three feet from the pin, and on our first day of real sunshine in weeks, I dragged a couple of clubs out of hibernation. Just slightly over the septic tank, on a small patch of bare ground between snowbanks, I coaxed a tee into the thawing remains of last year's grass. I lined up my best shot from a spot between two chipmunk craters 216' down the driveway to an imaginary flag just right of the mailbox. And as the blackbirds and chickadees became silent, I hauled off and hit the first ball of the season at Stonington. As if on a miraculous trajectory, it dropped to earth on the same spot the last ball(s) of the former season preferred—halfway from my imagined flag, but fully in the woods to the South. So skilled am I at placing the ball among the trees, I'm thinking perhaps I won't fight fate, and will, instead, go with what may be my special talent. I'll simply enjoy hitting a ball down the driveway on a nice day until the Gladstone Golf Club is plowed out . . . or the tick season begins in the woods.

13.5.9   Leaves of the Old Oak Tree

Halfway through the annual harvest, I remind myself hourly how much I love the big old oak trees surrounding my home. Even as I find a final resting place for last season's crop of leaves, acorns, and fallen twigs, fresh growth is budding along their branches. A whole new canopy of green will be in place before the children arrive this summer, and my family will enjoy the shade of these trees with me. The Provincetown hammock will swing again while overhead the harbor bell and chimes will have taken up the familiar wind songs. So, complain on about the yard work you people riding around on your yard groomers. I'm gathering each leaf with my dependable rake on these beautiful days and returning them all to the woods by wheelbarrow. This responsibility is not work to me. It is an exchange. And Henrik and I will sing: "I see the moon . . . down through the leaves of the old oak tree . . . ."

Yesterday the sun rose in a clear sky, filling my bedroom with a strange light I hadn't wakened to in months. At first I thought I had left a lamp on overnight. I then checked the clock, fearing I had really overslept and Auntie Carol, without our daily reassurance to each other, would have the paramedics on the way. But even before I crawled out from under the winter quilt, I could feel the new warmth in the room. While I slept away the final hours of winter, spring had arrived quietly during the night to surprise me in the morning.

13.5.17   SALSA SANDY

For my Sister, The Invincible Sandra Reta Rust Borg

Do you salsa, Sandy?
"Do I . . . what?" she laughed.
"Salsa. It's the music. I'm asking you to dance."
She'd had two margaritas when she pushed away her chair,
and, with citrus flavored courage, turned toward the voice.

At six months past divorce court,
when everything was "ex" . . .
the husband, house, a job, a town
her past in bins with curling tags,
the ship of dreams, gone worse for wear,
had slipped below the swells.
But buoyed by faith she surfaced
in calm and friendly seas
trailing a wake of Rubbermaid
and dog of dubious demeanor.
Tho some varieties wilt when uprooted,
those like Sandy, grab hold of possibility and bloom,
reflecting sunlight and color
in a new garden.

Thus, turning to her partner
was the Cha Cha Queen of Chaos,
The Tango Toots of Turmoil,
Mayhem's Mambo Mama,
saying: "Hell, kid, I can salsa
. . . . but now, each day's a waltz.".

13.5.13   Protective Custody

Just two days ahead of our latest snowstorm, I planted the apple tree which had been waiting in the garage, leaning against the wall in the darkness, its roots balled into an old bucket. As our wintry weather continued, I began speaking words of encouragement to it daily which grew to one-sided conversations about how wonderful spring and summer will be. People say that plants do better when you talk to them, and when the subject is optimism, people do better also. Occasionally I would hum a few bars of "The Sun Will Come Out Tomorrow . . . ." as I passed the tree, dragging the snow shovel out of retirement once more. And when "tomorrow" finally came, the tree and I were ready for it. Two trips to Menards had produced (4) 6 ft. stakes, one bag of premium garden soil, one top shelf trunk sleeve and enough deer repellant to drive the Stonington herds into Louisiana. I added a little chicken wire tied with colorful neck scarves. Through the window, I am admiring the brave little tree finally set free into U.P. soil . . . looking as if it is now in protective custody. I continue to talk to the little fellow every day as I examine it for signs of life. We are both hopeful.

13.5.29 For those fbf's who asked about my little apple tree, I am happy to report that, although we are a few seasons from the apple crop, it is showing great promise. Having recently survived 42 mph wind and frosty temperatures as well as my miserable gardening skills, the tree is alive with bursting buds . . . a testament to the assurance of new life in and around each of us. Get out there and bloom everyone . . . right where you are planted!

13.6.2   Mystery Trip

It was a small but adventuresome group of ladies who set out Monday on our Family and Community Education annual "Mystery Tour." We didn't have to drive far this year, but we traveled into another time and culture for a few hours. Sitting inside the large shelter constructed near Rapid River, we shared a fire with our Native American neighbors as they spoke of their customs and spirituality. When it was our turn to speak at the fire, a feather was passed to each of us. Many were too moved by the gathering to speak, but this, too, was customary. My friend Sparky and I left the shelter smoky, but eager to discuss what we had learned, and with hopes for the Dale Thomas Center which is organizing on the site. Considering all the mystique we became aware of, it was a fine mystery tour. I think my Dad's good friend Jimmy would be pleased to see me at the fire. He was full-blooded Chippewa . . . and half-hearted Baptist, he claimed.

13.6.9   The Dock

My neighbors discovered the water was too shallow for the new dock and lift for their pontoon boat. We all agreed the deeper water in front of my place was a better location. This is where their dock will be for the summer, lending some prestige to my shoreline. I like looking to the shoreline and seeing it there. The dock at Bay Mills was like a separate recreational area. We marked the beginning and ending of summer by hauling the old wooden sections in and out of the water. Before jetskis, water skis, four stroke outboards, we spent summer days catching minnows off the end of the dock, tying and untying the rope of the old Starcraft or just flat on our stomachs looking down into the water through the gaps between the boards. Some of our happiest daydreams, most satisfying peanut butter sandwiches, and best friends were there on the Bay Mills dock. Years later, I was surprised at how modest the size seemed when I stood at the end and looked back. But, when we were young, we were always looking forward . . . the dock and beyond stretched out endlessly through one warm and happy summer day after another.

13.6.26   Saving the Sofa

In 1972 I bought two large sofas which have been the backdrop for countless family photos. They followed me around for years, eventually settling down with me at Stonington. One met a tragic end some years ago, but the other, after undergoing major slipcover surgery, remains in the "tv room," still cozy and welcoming, now showing off the grandchildren and great-grandchildren My boys, who have sofas of their own now, still sink into its comfort and instantly relax into a total nap or lounge on it, full length, until bedtime. Fast Puppy stays with it all night, sleeping curled in the old blanket, his cell phone forgotten on the floor. Once I made a careless remark about buying a replacement. This idea was treated as if I had proposed giving away one of the grandchildren or the bulldog. A few days ago I removed the slipcovers, and, after years of attention from the drycleaners, placed them in the washer on "loving wash." This produced a mound of tattered material and snarled balls of threads. In a week, the boys would be coming from all corners of the country to find their familiar friend naked and pitifully aged. I sewed for 24 hours straight, reassembling the dignity of one of the family, which is now bright and smells of several laundry products. I want my children to keep all their happy memories, including . . . and especially . . . a comforting nap with an old friend in their mother's house.

13.7.20 anniecat, age 17 years, departed this morning for the Rainbow Bridge. She survived winter alone in the woods, outwitting predators, enduring cold and near starvation before finding the way to my door and into all our hearts. She was beautiful and loving to the end . . . .

13.7.10   Amy's Baby

Lance and Amy Golden have shared the good news. Their first child will be born in January. Amy put a little note on facebook yesterday, which right away brought (at last count) 65 comments. All of them told Amy what a wonderful mother she would be. This would be an immediate reaction from anyone who knows her. She has a gift for mothering . . . her family, friends, friends' families, children entrusted to her at daycare, any child that needs a tender hand. She is my dear granddaughter, and sometimes I have the urge to just lean against her comforting presence. We are all agreed . . . it is Amy's time to have her own child. Like everyone says: "She will be a wonderful mother!"

p.s. a few months later. It's a boy!! Lance William Golden III, at just a scooch under 8 lbs, born January 3, 2014, his grandmother Cherie's birthday.

13.7.14   Happy Birthday Beautiful Burba of Beaufort

Childhood, high school, college, forever friend Barb from Beautiful Beaufort by the Sea, SC is camping 8 miles down the road with husband, Earl. They have made this long trip so two old friends can acknowledge, together, their 80th year. Age has dictated the vigor and dignity of the celebrations, but cannot limit the joy of sharing a friendship which has brought us through nearly every imaginable situation. We are good for each other spiritually in the way only lifelong confidants can heartily praise successes or lighten the burden of guilt and sorrow with intimate wisdom. And when we look at each other, we have the delight of turning back the years.

> "***And yet we know that deep within
>
> We're winsome, bright and fair,
>
> Just as we were when we were young
>
> and life was ours to dare! . . ."
>
>   Anonymous, but definitely not Frank Yerby
>   Happy Birthday Barbara June from JoAnne Marie

13.7.30   Time Capsule

An interesting list of items went into Escanaba's time capsule, buried recently near the municipal dock, including: a small pump manufactured by EMP, a bottle of wine from Leigh's Garden Winery, Verizon cell phone, 2013 mint set, laminated one dollar bill, human rights campaign sticker and iron ore pellets, weekend edition of "Daily Press", menus from Culvers, Rosy's Diner, Stone House

and Wendy's, AT&T phone directories, telephone bill, list of Delta
County officials, a business directory . . . and we'll find Laurie Beggs
in the Delta-Schoolcraft ISD Directory. Also included: a Real Estate
Showcase booklet, community guide and two books on the area by
local authors, historical accounts from St. Francis Hospital and Bay
College, copy of Escanaba's city budget, a city utility bill, the city's
annual drinking water quality report, and local weather data. Finally,
in case a reminder is needed of what fun it was to fly at this time, a
sample boarding pass from Delta County Airport. I would have thrown
in a Pit Bull recording and my painful wedgie shoes. I think a can of
that great brew from the Keweenaw might have a chance of making
it to 2113. Certainly, the way things are going, whoever digs up the
capsule may need a beer.

13.7.31   Being Happy

Moll Doll, I was waiting for the coffee this morning and you just
jumped into my thoughts . . . like a little poke: "Hey gramma, you
haven't written to me for too long". I have been busy rounding off the
birthday festival . . . 30 days of celebrating my good fortune. Ryan
left this morning, and therefore I have been with all my children,
grandchildren and g-grandsons in the past days. Yes, I am indeed a
happy woman. The thing about family is how it keeps on growing and
the blessings multiply. Your new home with Phillip is as comforting
to all of your family as it is to you two. How wonderful to know you
are settling in to a new level of love and understanding. I am giving
some thought to my plans for the next decade, and so far have added
a brochure to the coffee table outlining Viking River Cruises, a trip
down the Danube by riverboat to Vienna where I would leap off and
live as a music librarian for the philharmonic until I had had my fill
of Strauss and Sachertorte. I might actually finish the little book, the
cover of which Darlene has created and the contents of which I have
finished editing and are so unworthy of the really fine cover. However,
I'm already doing the thing that makes me unspeakably happy and
gives life meaning . . . just being gramma. So, thank you dear Molly
for making me so glad to be who I am . . . love to you and Phillip . . .
jojo

13.8.1   Cabin Cake

Whenever I recall my childhood summers, a fat chunk of cake comes riding in on the happiest memories. Heavy with raisins and apples, rich with spice, the cake was iced with a generous layer of buttercream and brown sugar. This confection, itself, could bring world peace: Butter, whipping cream and brown sugar brought to boil before finishing with confectioner's sugar to a thick fudge. My mother began the recipe with an entire cup of oleo, which was a substitution for my grandmother's use of lard. Wanting to pass this recipe on to my children with FDA approval, I have come up with a mix of real sweet cream butter and Crisco in place of the margarine. The remaining preparation hasn't changed since Gram Sawyers checked the woodstove in the farm kitchen as she peeled up the cellar apples. Granulated white and dark brown sugars are beaten with the shortening, large fresh eggs and good vanilla before adding a cup of strong coffee which has been cooling. The usual cast of performers, flour, soda and salt, are mixed with a fragrant blend of cinnamon, nutmeg, ginger and cloves, then alternately blended into the batter with the apples and coffee. Allow the cake an hour in the oven as you enjoy the aroma of its apples and seasonings all through the house. I cannot smell that mixture of spices without a sense of happy anticipation.

We called it cabin cake. Its blue enamel pan wrapped in wax paper and old copies of "The Sault Evening News" was the last thing to go into the car trunk every trip we made to Bay Mills. Sitting atop the boxes of groceries, in company with our carefully packed paper bags of clothing and mother's freshly laundered towels and flannel blankets, it was, therefore, the first item carried through the door of the cabin. Part favorite treat, part good planning, the cabin cake was TRADITION. There would be no baking during our stay because we were without an oven. The rich cake in the old enamel pan stayed moist for days, and even a small portion was satisfying, lengthening its shelf life. In fact, cabin cake seemed to ripen with time and become even tastier . . . or was it that each day of swimming and jumping off the dock sharpened our appetites. Perhaps, too, such happiness with life makes all things, even a piece of cake, splendid.

13.8.2　Po

*** 04.7.10 I returned Monday from the Soo, where I attended the annual "Maritime Rose Parade" at Bay Mills. My sister, Patricia . . . or "Po" (nicknamed Rose) was the originator of the event. She loved having people at the Bay get together. By July of 1999 she knew that was to be her last summer at the cabin my parents had owned since we were babies. Jumping on a jetski on the 4th of July, weak from cancer and wearing a bandana instead of her trademark blond curly hair, she rode up and down the shoreline calling out to everyone to get in their boats and have a parade, then come back to the cabin for a party. Everyone did. She died three weeks before the next 4th of July, but the people at the Bay have continued the traditional boat parade, naming it for her. ***

When I reached the Rose Parade in the review of journals for my family, I was already aware that this was the first story that included my younger sister, Patricia (Po). She left us on June 6, 2000, and took great pieces of our hearts with her. It isn't as if she didn't leave us with a wealth of stories! Everyone who met her has some anecdote in which she played a part. My kids love to tell "Auntie Po" stories; and her children, Michael, Tammy and Todd, are able to recall her with affectionate laughter. She was certainly beautiful; and she had a sweet and generous nature that was appealing and yet . . . comfortable. I had no words to do her justice. People would say to me: "If only Pat could see this." And I would remind them that she has the best seat in the house. To me, she is always just out there, drifting in one of the old inner tubes off the dock at Bay Mills, holding onto the other for me. And every time the Silver Bullet Band plays "Old Time Rock and Roll" . . . we all dance.

13.8.4　Trinity Lutheran Celebration

"Trinity Lutheran—a white beacon of Christianity—today stands tall and strong on the limestone cliff of Stonington. Its walls were twice built with wood cut by its members, it was built with volunteer labor, and it is full of the love and the pride of a job well done. It is a symbol of 100 years of Christian tradition and of the loving, caring people of Stonington who made homes in a . . . wilderness and made a church for the greater worship of God . . . ." John C. Hager

Today our "little white church in the wildwood" celebrates 100 years of Christian faith and community on Stonington (a location described by the Lutheran Bishop as "the Synod's longest cul-de-sac"). In a special service at the church, its congregation and visitors will hear stories from our most senior members and former clergy. I'm thinking the Scripture will be read from those passages all Lutherans take personally. Annie has prepared a beautiful prelude and favorite hymns, her little feet treading the familiar path she has worn between piano and organ. Other musical offerings will be made by members who share their voices every Sunday to bolster the wobbly singing and enthusiasm of the congregation during hymns suspiciously non-Lutheran. Vicar Diane will bring it all together with her conviction and infectious faith.

Following worship, the celebration will continue at the Township Hall, a short drive down the road. The Ladies Aid has promised no less than 28 various salads to embellish the tables, and the area's famous coffee will flow freely. When the cakes have been reduced to crumbs and the stories have shortened, the Annual Women's Association Raffle will be held, distributing the 52 prizes which have been piling up in Carl and Ginny Dahlin's garage. The raffle is no afterthought. For years, Ginny has spearheaded this project, collecting, printing, selling to bring in amounts which account for nearly all the Ladies Aid budget. So, this is a special Sunday in Stonington, but it is also typical. This is exactly what Jesus had in mind when he called for a community of faith.

13.8.21   The Pleasure of Their Company

The new season of ground cover has begun. While my Sister, Sandy, rakes up her maple leaves in the Soo, we are being pelted by the first small acorns from the oaks which monopolize the tree population on Squaw Point. Such small missiles can startle you into wakefulness at night as they bounce off the roof. A quiet read on the deck is painfully interrupted, and visitors enjoying an outdoor toddy must fish the falling debris from their drinks. We are just moving into another season of stuff that drops from overhead. No sooner has the fallen snow melted, revealing layers of sodden leaves, branches and gazillions of acorns (aren't the squirrels and deer supposed to eat these??), the serious shedding begins: puffy stuff from the birches, followed by little catkins and "helicopter" pods from the maples. Somewhere in between, each petal from the blossoms on the flowering crab and cherry will drift into clumps on my struggling lawn. Just before the snow comes again, my little world in the woodland will give a great sigh and the entire season of leaves and acorns will fall to earth to wait for spring.

I am a visitor here . . . these old oaks and maples are sharing their estate with me. For the pleasure of their company and for the beauty they bring to my days, I will tidy things up a bit for them once in a while.

13.9.30   Last Day of September

I am forwarding to you a part of a perfectly beautiful day here on Stonington, such as: 1. I saw a gigantic hornet in the garage this a.m. as I was loading the car to leave for quilting. Good luck . . . it didn't get into the car with me, but flew over and pasted itself to the side window next to me. It was a race down 513 as I tried to dislodge it from the window. Glancing to my left every few minutes during the wild ride, I saw the hornet still clinging to the glass. This left me to begin planning my escape from the car without allowing it into the car or unto me at journey's end. When the car came to a stop, the dazed hornet slid off the window and crawled into hiding in the grass. Sort of the same exit most of my passengers make. 2. Returning home, a monster size porcupine crossed the road just ahead of me and was lumbering toward the woods on my left. I stopped, rolled down the window and made my little chirping sounds (used for chipmunks, deer, squirrels, all bird species). The big guy stopped, turned around and listened, then began to walk toward me. I don't know if he wanted to be friendly or aggressive because I felt I should drive on, but the thing is I talked to a porcupine this morning who paused beside the edge of the glorious fall woodlands to communicate with me.

13.10.13   Jo Meets Jo

I'm told that if something frightens you, it should not be left behind you to lurk around back there. Turn and take a good look. Situations . . . and people . . . can be greatly improved by giving your imagination a rest. And so, at 1:15 this morning I was in front of my not-so-wide screen, with every light in the house on, to watch Jo Nesbo's first appearance on U.S. talk tv. I read only one of his novels; and after the bad dreams that resulted, it is my nature to wonder about the creator of such narrative and characters. Looking like a regular from "Mad Men" (which was strangely comforting), Nesbo talked about his other life as member of a Norwegian rock group and revealed that he has written a children's book (Yikes!). Showing a wonderful sense of humor, he then sent me off to bed with that good memory of him to dilute any further nightmares from his book . . . that, and a good laugh over the realization that the name of a main character in his books translates to Harry Hole. With Harry and his other creations so popular in over 40 countries, I hope Nesbo makes more tv appearances. A lot of sleepless readers are out there . . . .

13.10.21   Scott's Socks

When I was working full-time, my children helped with the laundry; but, I had to do my part, too. Sometimes my quality time with the washer/dryer began after the family was fast asleep in their last pair of clean jammies. Saving the worst for last one night, the boys' socks were being downloaded . . . in particular, Scott's red fashion statements . . . when something bit my hand. With the washer already filling, I couldn't see anything swimming in the suds, but after closing the washer, I also closed the door to the laundry room and fled. My hand was already swollen and still swelling. With the fatigue that a job plus four children often brings on, I went to bed with my hand in a bag of ice, leaving a note on the kitchen table saying I had been bitten by Scott's sock; and in case I "died in my sleep" they should call the office for me in the morning. Fortunately, I'm here to finish this story and can reveal that the culprit was a large black and white striped hornet. When the wet wash was removed the next morning, the drowned hornet was still clinging to a red sock. It must have loved those socks as much as Scott. He still has to defend himself when his brothers tease him with: "Yeah, well, our socks never bit Mom."

13.10.25   October

Winter is looming when I put a runner on the deck. Each year the sturdy strip of carpet comes out of a corner in the garage to make its announcement that snow and ice are on the way. With a borrowed stapler, I fasten the runner along the lines of punctures from previous years, making certain its edges won't be lifted by weeks of shoveling. Somehow, each fall the old carpet manages to look fresh . . . and reassuring. It keeps us from sliding off the deck and into physical therapy. Today there is a mixed message just outside the door. The geraniums still bloom profusely and bravely in the pots now sitting on the first sign of winter.

These first cold days and there is a scent of chili in the air. My friends claim they all have a hunger for a good bowl of chili and are cooking up the hamburg and beans in great pots. At my house it is spareribs and sauerkraut. My Dad passed on a lot of the German Genes to his oldest daughter . . . His favorite meal was a pot of pork hocks with or without the kraut. In the winter, after simmering all day on the back of the stove, After adding a generous amount of garlic cloves, the pot of meat was set out on the garage steps overnite where it jellied and was eaten with a splash of good vinegar and lots of pepper. Spareribs were a little "high cut" for the butcher's family, so we ate the hocks or what is now called "country ribs." My meal is cooking in a crockpot, and the house is filled with the familiar fragrance and the comforting presence of all those memories of my family and a pot of pork and kraut.

13.11.26   Thanksgiving

This afternoon I drove home from Escanaba in our first snowstorm. The turkey (thank you Jeff and Laurie) rode safely in the trunk, surrounded by the ingredients for the side dishes which will accompany him to dinner on Thursday. As the wind battled my mighty Honda, I was trying to come up with a "rant" about winter arriving too soon. I see that rants are very popular on the internet, and I thought I should maybe try to compose one; but complaining about the weather will never change it. I leave to the experts the real rant issues such as improvement for our government, for humanity in general or maybe even for us Packer fans. By the time I reached my driveway's first snowdrift, I had turned my thinking around. Instead of ranting against those things I cannot change, I'll hope to always be involved in a more useful way . . . and will be thankful for so many blessings, such as a safe ride home through the storm for the turkey and me with a trunkful of holiday favorites to share with my family. Have a Happy Thanksgiving!!

13.12.1   Ceilings

My childhood room was upside down.
On the ceiling plaster swirled,
creating seas of whitecaps.
Fat stars sparkled on the linoleum.
As I grew up, the waves calmed to ripples,
stars dimming from wear
and mother's diligent scrubbing.

On summer nights at the cabin,
the old boards of the porch roof came alive.
Knotholes floated, shaped and merged
as oil lamps made the shadows move,
and bears danced overhead.
They're there yet, in the ceiling,
hiding from electric light.

Lying on the permafrost, encased in down,
I tried to sleep in vernal twilight.
Tents have no dark corners there in June;
my thin nylon ceiling a fragile hindrance
to the Midnight Sun and marauding wildlife
while camping on the Ketchimak.

Heat from the woodstove stayed below.
only whiffs of smoke from the fire,
with scent of cedar drifted up the stairs.
But waters warm as Sargasso filled the bed
in the room under the eaves
where corner to corner overhead
the insulation claimed CERTAINTEED.

13.12.28   Winter

Much like us chilled Yoopers, our daily dose of snow appears to be
half-hearted about winter this morning. In recent days of sub-zero
temperatures, the snow didn't really fall on us through all that frigid
air. Traveling on the cruel wind from the north, it blew in from
Canada, creating mountainous banks across the entire U.P. and
polishing the roadways to menacing, icy perfection.

Today there is no wind, and with the temperature hovering at heat wave readings above zero, the snow arrives in a lazy mist, drifting over the ice of Bay de Noc. The opposite side of the bay is not visible, but close to my shore the outlines of two fish shacks appear. In the coming weeks, the shacks will multiply in clusters like mushrooms, spreading further out onto the bay as the ice thickens, merging in areas into small communities atop the water. As winter closes us off from parts of our world for a time, it provides, on pathways of ice and snow, the way to another.

SMALL THINGS

Have you seen the Bay de Noc shoreline anywhere?? Did it leave for South Carolina and become part of Battery Creek?? Last weekend the water in our bay went WAY out again . . . and didn't come back. We are becoming more than suspicious up here. The week preceding we had 4 days of rain which should have raised the water level on our shorelines at least as high as the puddles running across US-2. We have ruled out Facebook and texting, two favorite choices when looking at what's wrong with the world. Some of us want to blame the Democrats and will be getting together our own campaign ad urging redistribution of water resources. (Watch for airings on pirate TV out of Trenary).

This morning Tom and I are going into town together to pick up some things at Menards; and I hope he doesn't cramp my style in my favorite store. The possibilities for fruitful encounters are limitless in the shingles and siding departments this time of year. If you linger by the loading area, I've found, you can get a good idea of which candidates have the nicer trucks.

Jeff is hunting ducks out front as I write this. Shooting going on, so hope he's having some success. My neighbors from the camp across the road are here for the bow season; and their daughter-in-law shot a nice deer close to my backyard. Something ate a partridge just behind my garage, but left me the feathers. I feel like I am dealing with game management situations.

This morning a rabbit came to my slider door and peered in the window at me. There sat a picture-book creature, a pure cottontail bunny richly furred against the cold. Its large round eyes studied me while the perfect nose, twitched delicately. So unspoiled, and too young to realize this sort of contact was not acceptable. Therefore, we just sat and looked at each other, appreciating the encounter. I thought of putting out a special treat, but remembered it is rabbit season on Squaw Point, and it is best not to encourage my new friend to leave the safety of the woods.

My cell phone staged a protest, allowing me to send and receive, but refusing to display calls or alerts on the screen. I imagined the voicemail lady sounding a tad grumpy with me for relying on her to constantly recite missed calls. Calling out was risky without the numbers on the screen. Note to Self: Remove Johnny Depp from speed dial. He didn't believe I was really trying to call my chiropractor.

My friend Donna likes to iron everything, but admits she is not faithful to the task. In a marathon of ironing recently she set the bottom of the clothes basket as a goal. Upon reaching it, she discovered the last item down there was daughter Pam's brownie uniform. Pam is now over 40.

I'm signed up to bring soup to the church on the 13th. The soup is prepared and in Mosher's freezer. They will begin thawing it in case I miss my connection Tuesday night in Detroit. It's the Lutheran Way. I was thinking about the story of Lorna Javenkoski who was in a collision with a truck, and called from her hospital bed to tell Carol her salad was prepared for a church supper, and would Carol have someone go to the house and make sure it was taken to the hall. Is it a sacred thing pledging "a dish to pass" at Trinity? I know that most of the recipes are truly divine.

I am the Bulldog Shouter. Shouting seems to work as well as whispering with Muggins. No wonder Jeff wanted that dog . . . they both have some of the traits I recall in him as a teenager. During that stage I was a Jeff Shouter.

Garden Notes: The deer are decimating my garden; but, it's almost like a mercy killing because my attempts at gardening leave small plants struggling for survival. What actually grows are my evergreens. The two by the garage, trimmed with my rusty hedge shears, have received comment on their resemblance to bonsai plantings. With rain everyday this week, we are about under water. I finally have all my petunias planted, but wonder if I should have put in water lilies.

It is the last weekend in April, and there is an iceberg large enough to sink an ore boat just sitting there a few feet from my beach. Two eagles are perched on top as if they had booked a cruise on the top deck.

This morning, both my daughters-in-law are at their finest. Each, under separate circumstances, facing the brunt of fear and helplessness for us. Pam has suffered and rejoiced with granddaughter Kaylee for years without losing faith, a steadfast presence for her son and the entire family. Laurie's devotion to the welfare and happiness of her family and anyone or anything that touches it is legendary. Although today I am anxious, I am reminded of these two beautiful women and how blessed we are to have them.

Seven a.m. in an April downpour. Friend Darlene and I are digging out our rain jackets and heading for Marquette. Since January, we have cancelled this trip three times, watching the Kohls sales come and go and valuable Younkers coupons expire one by one. It is as if the weather gods look at our calendars and plan a blizzard or "severe" precipitation of some sort.

All my grandchildren within arms' reach these past days . . . each face precious, each voice music. Molly and I couldn't say goodbye last night, and she packed to go back to Richmond, crying. I said goodbye to Amy, both of us in tears and unable to say words anymore. I couldn't say goodbye to Ryan, so I walked down to the beach to watch him and Tom spashing around together, my two puppies in the water, then drove home to be alone again. I feel ungrateful because I'm so sad when they leave, knowing I should be happy for these days of laughter and being able to watch and hear them with all this love.

Dear Facebook Friends: I am still receiving all those pop-up advertising cures for wrinkles and belly fat. Add to that the recent ads for Single Yooper Women With Wrinkles And Belly Fat Match.com, and I am beginning to suspect my facebook page has been hacked. Should I check "in a relationship" and put a cute puppy photo on my profile? I'm so not good with this. I used to write letters on flowered onionskin using a pen filled with purple ink.

I had hoped for all of us to have a cyber visit when the gang was here, but that day is a blur in my memory. I had 15 for dinner and two dogs under the tables. A few drop-ins added to the merriment. By then my Clay Matthews shirt was speckled with whatever I cooked and steam from my new Paula Deen cookware had done bad things to my holiday hairdo. Just as well you didn't have to see me like that. Nothing more heartbreaking than a soiled and bedraggled Smelt Goddess. I am reading on my Kindle, but so far all I have read is how to read on a Kindle. This is what we would call a "beautiful" winter day. This new tolerance for winter weather may result from the waning enthusiam over sunny decks on a cruise ship. Since Kim and I have a stateroom somewhere behind the engine room, the divers would leave us there if the captain runs us aground.

At my age, I am grateful to still be included when the conversation turns to running marathons, walking 3 miles a day or soul cycling. So when the subject of shoes came up, I tucked my tattered Earth brands under the chair and shared the news of my quest for the perfect shoes . . . miracle footwear which would radiate comfort and confidence upward to my undependable ankles, knees, hips and back. I need a magical cross-trainer for my event: Menard's parking lot to their paint department. Hopefully, I will be able to improve my stamina and pace enough to take in the seasonal and electrical sections.

A wonderful day of transition to Fall. Sunny but cool. The house smells of my first pot of chili since last season. Jeff and Tommy are just down the road making a woodpile; and I have had my Saturday "fireside chats" with Kim and Bumbie. I will begin putting the beach chairs away and the boys and I will move part of the wood pile to the lakeside deck for easy access when the snowdrifts form. These times make me stop and think about how many more years I will be preparing for another winter. Then these familiar chores become comforting.

Sometime during the night the snow stopped falling. These past windless days, we lived in total whiteness as hour after hour it floated down . . . unrelenting. All shapes and forms surrendered and peacefully slipped beneath the drifts. There is stillness and a world of perfectly level snow all around us this morning. Looking across the bay, the outline of the frosted treeline gives slight contrast to a dazzling landscape. The darkening sky beyond only adds depth and drama to this winter "still life . . . ."

FINIS

Always remember the realization that moved you to write. It is good to be able to look back and remember good times and learn from the bad ones. It is exciting to look forward with purpose and hope. But, to live in the moment is elegant. Absorbing and storing up experiences provides a feast to last your lifetime. I have seen faces and scenes from moments so beautiful and happy that I want to "fill up my eyes" with them. Fill up your eyes, open your heart, be limitless.

Acknowledgement

Of course, thank you to Barbara Prohazka Larson for the years of friendship and for the email which inspired this book. Anyone who reads it will know that years and distance were unable to diminish the depth or spirit of that friendship. BFF Darlene N. Prokos created the enchanting cover, the most artistic element of my project. And thank you Dan (Deej) Beggs who stepped in when my laptop and I were in simultaneous meltdown and helped put all the words safely in cyber space.

Joan Rust

CPSIA information can be obtained at www.ICGtesting.com
Printed in the USA
LVOW08s1434220215

427891LV00001B/292/P